Barbara Brown MA

Brodie's Notes on Flora Thompson's

Lark Rise to Candleford

Pan Books London and Sydney

To the student

A close reading of the set book is the student's primary task. These Notes will help to increase your understanding and appreciation of the book, and to stimulate *your own* thinking about it; *they are in no way intended as a substitute* for a thorough knowledge of the book.

First published 1978 by Pan Books Ltd
Cavaye Place, London SW10 9PG
3 4 5 6 7 8 9

ISBN 0 330 50124 0
Filmset in Great Britain by
Northumberland Press Ltd, Gateshead, Tyne and Wear
Printed and bound by
Richard Clay (The Chaucer Press) Ltd, Bungay, Suffolk

Contents

Page references are to the Penguin Modern Classics edition of *Lark Rise to Candleford*, but as references are also given to individual chapters the Notes may be used with any edition of the book.

The setting of *Lark Rise to Candleford*

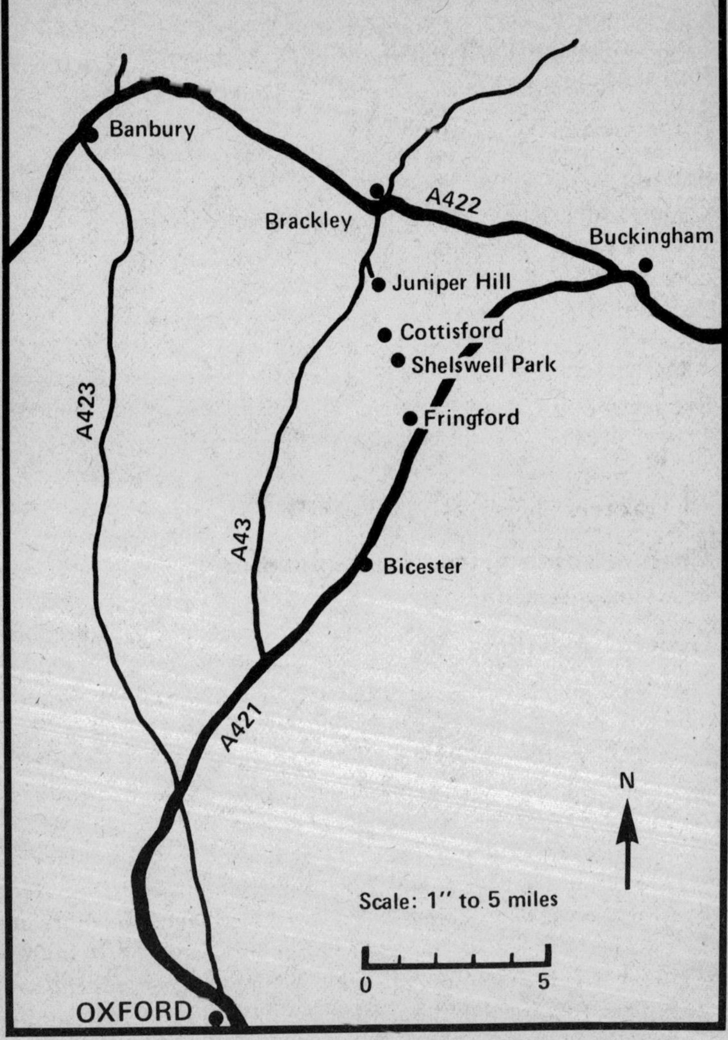

The author and her work

What is known of Flora Thompson's life is largely derived from a reading of her books and from the research carried out by Margaret Lane, first published in the *Cornhill* and later in *Purely for Pleasure* (1966).

Flora Thompson was born Flora Jane Timms on 5 December 1876 in Juniper Hill in north-east Oxfordshire, the eldest child of a large family. Her father Albert Timms was a stonemason from Oxford who had settled in the hamlet while engaged on some local work; his wife Emma had been a nursemaid at a nearby rectory. Flora left home at fourteen to take up a position as an assistant at the Post Office at Fringford, run at that time by a Mrs Whitton, an old friend of her mother's. In her late teens she worked in several post offices as a temporary assistant before taking up a more permanent post at Grayshott, near Hindhead, Surrey. In 1900 she met John Thompson, a young post office clerk from Aldershot, and they married when he was transferred to the main post office at Bournemouth. His further promotions to sub-postmaster and postmaster took the family (which in time included three children) first to Liphook, Hampshire (1916), then to Dartmouth (1938). When John Thompson retired in 1940 they settled in Brixham, and it was there that Flora Thompson died in 1947.

Her background was hardly sympathetic to the aspiring writer, although, recalling her childhood in *Lark Rise to Candleford*, she describes how she was encouraged to learn to read at an early age to avoid having to go to school, as her father had always intended to move from the hamlet (Chapter 2, p.43). But what set out to be merely the acquisition of a practical skill to placate the education authorities soon became a compulsive habit. Her constant reading of anything she could lay her hands on, either in her own home or in the homes of neighbours, caused talk in the hamlet; her early attempts at verse, inspired by the alliterative lines of Scott's nature poems, which she showed to her mother in an 'unguarded moment', led to a lecture later that evening on her poor needlework and a reminder that 'You can't *afford* to waste your time' (Chapter 24, p.333). To some extent an account of her work is an account of her growing confidence in her considerable gifts as a creative artist, and an increasing sense of conviction of the necessity for their imaginative expression in literary form. Not everything she wrote has been published, although the Oxford University Press are bringing out more of her work. The following outline is a guide to titles available at the moment. Her early poetry is not easily obtainable and the quotations provided in this Study Aid may help to provide an overall view of the way her ideas and interests developed.

Despite early criticism Flora Thompson never really stopped writing. With the newspaper and magazine market in mind, she tried her hand at many forms, including verse, sketches and romantic fiction. Her work appeared in leading dailies before and after the First World War (Chapter 35, p.467), and through similar channels she became friendly with the Scottish writer Ronald Campbell Macfie, who encouraged her more serious literary ambitions, at that time in the field of poetry. In 1921 Philip Allan and Company brought out a slim volume of her poems, *Bog-Myrtle and Peat*, with a dedicatory poem to Macfie that acts as a statement of the kind of poet she saw herself to be, as opposed to Macfie:

> Yours are the moors, the billowy seas,
> Tall mountains and blue distances.
> Mine is a cottage garden, set
> With marigold and mignonette,
> And all the wildling things that dare,
> Without a gardener's fostering care.
> Yet very well-content I rest
> In my obscure, sequestered nest;
> For from my cottage garden I
> Can see your cloud-peaks pierce the sky!

It is interesting to see the writer cast herself so early in the role of the quiet observer of the lowly natural scene, while at the same time she puts no limits on the range of vision of the 'onlooker' figure. The review of the volume in *The Times Literary Supplement* (17 March 1921) gave her modest praise as a nature poet: 'A passion for the open English country – a keen receptiveness to its sights and sounds are the notes of the pieces collected in this slim volume, and they are given adequate and tasteful expression.' Themes other than that of nature, and of interest to the reader of her later work are the nostalgic yearning for the past, as in the poems 'You have forgotten our Cave' and 'Wild Thyme': ('A scent of wild-thyme on the air/Can bear one back to days afar'); and a statement of belief in the value of simple pleasures, as in 'The Earthly Paradise' ('I desire no heaven of gold harps/Give me the harps of earth'). The latter theme is given more directly anti-intellectual expression in the poem 'Moments of Vision', where she juxtaposes thought and feeling as negative and positive values:

> I read last night the words of one –
> That master among men
> Who holds this life a cramping cage,
> The grave our goal. And then
> O'er my hushed senses stole the scent
> Of hedgerows sweet with rain,
> And children's happy laughter rent
> The soft Spring dusk in twain.

Finally, there is the theme of undeclared or unfulfilled love, couched in highly romantic terms; for example, the poem addressed 'To One in Prison' which begins 'Had I the power to match my love . . .'

In 1924, because of her poetic interests, Flora Thompson founded the Peverel Society, a postal writing club that lasted for some years. Selected contributions were published under the title of *The Peverel Book of Verse*, advertised on the back cover as 'The Peverel Monthly, a monthly magazine for all who can write or wish to learn to do so.' There are two copies in the British Library, dated January 1928 and September 1929, and the title-pages inform readers that the contents have been 'selected and arranged by Flora Thompson'.

In the late 1930s she began to write sketches about her childhood – for example, 'Old Queenie' and 'May Day', which were published in *The Lady* and *The Fortnightly Review* (p.20 in *Purely for Pleasure*). She was encouraged by the Oxford University Press to expand these writings into a book and the result was *Lark Rise* (1939), which was an instant success. A note prefacing that edition, and the reprint of 1940, describes the work as she saw it: 'This book tells of the life in an Oxfordshire hamlet in the 'eighties. The drawings were made by Mr Lynton Lamb in the village around which the story is written. The setting has remained unchanged since the period described by the author.' It was reviewed by *The Times Literary Supplement* (13 May 1939) under the heading of 'Social History' and praised for its 'vivid memory and faithful portrayal of a way of life that has almost passed'. She was urged by her publishers to write a follow-up, and *Over to Candleford* appeared in 1941. Flora Thompson was at pains to emphasize in the prefatory note that the work was not intended to be simply autobiographical and that she aimed in her reminiscences to cover a wider canvas than the purely personal: 'The following is intended less as autobiography than as a record of the impressions of a child brought up in a remote country hamlet in the eighteen-eighties. It is written in the third person because the writer can best see objectively, across the gulf of time and war and change, the child who was herself moving in that now vanished world.' The book was praised for maintaining the high standard set in *Lark Rise*, and Flora Thompson for her ability to distil the 'very essence of English life, faithful embroidery on the larger pattern of English history' (*The Times Literary Supplement*, 12 July 1941). *Candleford Green* soon followed in 1943, written with great difficulty during air raids, and was even more popular than its predecessors.

The three books were reissued as a trilogy, *Lark Rise to Candleford*, in 1945, with an introduction by H. J. Massingham and illustrated with wood-engravings by Judith Neild. There have been many reprints.

The reviewer of *Candleford Green* had concluded, 'We wait, as the publisher's note says, impatient for the next instalment.' (*The Times Literary Supplement*, 13 March 1943.) There *was* a 'next instalment' which carried Laura's story a little further – the book *Heatherly* – but it has had to wait a long time for publication, as apparently Flora Thompson was dissatisfied with it.

Her final work, *Still Glides the Stream*, was finished a few weeks before she died in 1947. The book is set in a village, Restharrow, at the end of the nineteenth century (as was *Candleford Green*), and events are viewed mainly in the third person through the eyes of the child Charity, who is drawn on similar lines to Laura. The book begins with Charity, now a middle-aged schoolteacher living away from the district, returning to the haunts of her youth and reflecting on the changes that have taken place. But after the opening sections the book develops into a novel in which realistically represented characters are not merely recalled but are given some room to grow through experience and interaction. There are many parallels, in its general conception, with Mrs Gaskell's *Cranford* and, in plot and characterization, with George Eliot's *Adam Bede* and *Middlemarch*.

Charity, an only child, spends much of her time with her family of cousins who live on a nearby farm where their father is bailiff. He has many traits in common with Uncle Tom of Candleford, demonstrating a combination of good workmanship, sturdy independence of outlook, generosity and individuality – qualities which George Eliot found in her own father and commemorated in the character of Caleb Garth in *Middlemarch*, and Adam Bede in the novel of that name. Another interesting link is the presentation of the enigmatic Stella Pocock, the secret writer of the poison-pen letters that set off a chain of events in the village, with near tragic results for the innocent Mrs Burdett. As with Rosamond Vincey in *Middlemarch*, her fair, cold beauty attracts a nature warmer than her own, and she marries Charity's soldier-cousin, Oliver.

A final link is perhaps more revealing, for Flora Thompson diverges from George Eliot in social attitude in her presentation of the pretty farm-girl, Bess. A situation potentially similar to that in *Adam Bede* (where Hetty Sorrel, the milkmaid, is seduced by Arthur Donnithorne, the Squire's nephew, with tragic repercussions), is outlined in *Still Glides the Stream*. The friendship that develops between Bess and Roger Maitland, the young lord of the Manor, becomes a topic for village gossip, fanned by Stella's poison-pen letters, and causes his mother to visit the farm in high dudgeon. But Bess is fashioned by her author in a different mould from that of poor vain Hetty Sorrel. Though hurt by the general malice of Mrs Maitland's attack on her, she is amazed that anybody could seriously think that she would allow herself to become emotionally involved with the young squire, not because of any sense of her social inferiority, but because she has looked at him with the eyes of an equal and found him wanting. Her attitude has, in fact, more in common with the independence of mind found in Lawrence's working-class heroines and with 20th-century liberated ladies than with any earlier female characterization of that social class. From the point of view of plot, the interesting development is that Mrs Maitland is told to mind her own business by Uncle Reuben, particularly over her suggestion that she will find a 'place' for Bess away from the district, and it is Roger Maitland who leaves the area for the West Indies. Despite her broadly based sympathy for all the characters she presents, here, as elsewhere when class conflict arises, Flora Thompson leaves the reader in no doubt as to whose side she is on.

Flora Thompson's popularity shows no signs of abating. The National Theatre production of *Lark Rise* at the Cottesloe which began in March 1978 was an instant sell-out for the seventeen performances scheduled. This dramatization, which had an enthusiastic critical reception, was written by Keith Dewhurst and based mainly on the first part of the trilogy. It concentrated on one day in the life of the hamlet (in the manner of Dylan Thomas's *Under Milk Wood*), beginning with the children from the end house going mushrooming in the early morning, through scenes in the hamlet's day in the field and homes, and ending with the gathering at the inn that evening. It was a 'promenade production', the audience mingling with the actors around the cheap-jack's stall or Jerry Parish's fish-cart, and audience participation in some of the games and dances.

Further reading

The Education of the People, May Sturt (Routledge and Kegan Paul)

Written for Children: Outline of English Language, John Rowe Townsend (Penguin)

Victorian England: Portrait of an Age, G. M. Young (OUP)

Culture and Society 1780–1950, Raymond Williams (Penguin)

The Country and the City, Raymond Williams (Paladin)

The Uses of Literacy, Richard Hoggart (Penguin)

Approach

Raymond Williams includes *Lark Rise to Candleford* in the category of 20th-century country writing – part memoir, part record – to which belong the works of George Sturt (George Bourne) (*The Wheelwright's Shop* and *Change in the Village*), George Ewart Evans (*Ask the Fellows Who Cut the Hay* and *The Pattern under the Plough*) and, more recently, Ronald Blythe (*Akenfield*). This genre has certain recurrent features.

The basic approach is a detailed reconstruction of a rural England of the past, with autobiography and record intermingled. The past is described as a Golden Age, the present despaired of, and country and urban life are set in opposition as symbols of innocence and corruption. Raymond Williams also describes how the harking back to 'Old England' as something in the recent past has in fact been a recurrent feature of English Literature from Langland's *Piers Plowman* through to Goldsmith's *The Deserted Village* (1769) and William Cobbett's *Rural Rides* (1830). Novels of the second half of the nineteenth century such as George Eliot's *Mill on the Floss* (1860) and Thomas Hardy's books written between 1871 and 1896 'look back' in time and link the passing of the rural life of 'Old England' with the effects of the Industrial Revolution.

Lark Rise to Candleford is a work of considerable literary importance because of the imaginative force of Flora Thompson's recall of the past, the presentation of which is the main concern of this Study Aid. Far from its being the artless warbling of her 'native wood-notes wild' (to quote Milton on Shakespeare), the author makes it clear to us in her interruptions to the text that this celebration of the pastoral scene was intended as a serious work, with a distinct moral purpose. By presenting a detailed record in social and human terms, Flora Thompson wished to demonstrate that life before the turn of the century in rural areas had a quality which she felt had been subsequently lost. Her appeal is directed primarily to the heart rather than the head, and the work speaks powerfully to the city dweller's nostalgia for the rural past; here, with a consummate artistry, a vanished world is re-created in depth.

Life then, the author claims at the end of Chapter 3, was happier, though in many ways harder. She makes no secret of the poverty; details which reveal the harshness of the life are used as background to add to the essential grit of her characters, and in this way realism is combined with nostalgia in her approach. She did not write to arouse indignation for the plight of the agricultural poor – she expected the reader's admiration for the people portrayed, not his pity. Even though conditions were against them, she argues, people in the past were capable of cheerfulness and stoicism. Men whistled and sang on their daily round, though they knew that only a narrow line divided them from the homeless poor who swarmed the countryside; that sickness meant no pay; and that old age meant the workhouse. They enjoyed their work in the fields and the satisfaction of getting in the harvest, even though the older workers had limbs crippled and distorted by the rheumatism that was an inevitable consequence of a working life spent in the open, and though their share of the harvest money was a pittance. The women were forced to rely on parcels of clothes sent from daughters in service to dress themselves and their families; nevertheless they took pride in their appearance and in their skill in re-shaping these cast-off garments, as well as caring for large families in houses without running water or indoor sanitation. 'Better be out of the world than out of the fashion' was one of their more frequent sayings (Chapter 6, p.102).

Though she wrote with a serious purpose, Flora Thompson's work is not solemn, for she was anxious to show that life was then far more enjoyable. Pleasure in living in the face of devastating odds, good humour, racy speech, neighbourly conduct, pride in a job well done – these are the traditional peasant virtues which are being celebrated. Yet, at the same time, she remembers with deep affection the people she knew, not as cardboard symbols of rustic fulfilment, but as real people. It was little wonder that her work was so delightedly received by a country at war, for she portrays an essentially indomitable race.

Her targets for satire are principally those too uncaring or self-centred to share, or even comprehend, her generous approach to life, in particular the socially pretentious or those of church or state whose self-imposed task it is to keep the peasantry in their place. (See the section on *Characters*.) It is of interest that, of her family, her father – townsman, radical and intellectual – is presented as one who is eventually destroyed by his vision. Her mother's social ambitions are always viewed quizzically and tolerantly. Edmund, however, the soldier-poet, is a man of the land, the epitome of peasant integrity and sterling worth. Her social view, in fact, looks constantly backwards throughout the trilogy to a more ideal 'feudal' world where people belonged – her true heroes are the peasants (the people of Lark Rise), the craftsmen (Uncle Tom, Miss Lane and her men at the forge) and the aristocracy (Sir Timothy and Lady Adelaide). But as Laura moves away from Lark Rise and the autobiographical element becomes prominent, the changing social scene and manners of the day are often satirically presented.

Nobody is treated too harshly throughout the trilogy – with the possible exception of poor Mrs Green of Candleford Green, the symbol of suburban sterility – for Flora Thompson's is a world where people are essentially well-meaning if occasionally misguided. Though the settings are similar to those of Hardy's Wessex, her approach is in direct contrast to his, for she consistently avoids the dark passions that move men, as well as any suggestion of emotional depths. There is, for example, no deliberate cruelty in her view of life – look at the presentation of the episode in *Lark Rise* where the old Major is taken against his will to the workhouse. The doctor and the attendant are sympathetically presented – they were acting in his best interests: 'They were right in their decision' (5,89), though she suggests they were insensitive in view of his nature and spirit. Similarly, the children who bullied her on the way to school and tormented the old tramp 'did not mean to be cruel'; and she excuses them on the grounds that they were 'strong, hardy children, without much imagination, and overflowing with energy and high spirits which had to find an outlet' (23,320). Elsewhere the general indifference to the sufferings of animals, shown in the pig-killings, and in the birds'-nesting (9,152); and the prejudice displayed towards any group that was 'different', is explained as ignorance that could be corrected by education, not as evidence of man's intrinsic hardness of heart.

Lark Rise to Candleford offers many things to the reader – a re-creation of a vanished world; unforgetable character portraits; humour and satire; the beauty of a fine prose style; and a remarkable sensibility in the character of Laura. Whether Flora Thompson convinces the reader that life then really was more golden, and that the pleasures outweighed the pains in the way she suggests, is a matter for the individual to decide. Paradoxically, she was perhaps, too fine an artist to be totally successful as a polemicist in the way she had hoped to be; and the scene she presents is sufficiently complex to be open to more than one interpretation. Finally, though she constantly reminds the reader that she is writing of the past and that dark days are upon us, the people are so real and the total experience so compulsive, that the message that none of this any longer applies is quite at odds with the spirit of the book. If we trust the tale and not the teller, there we find constant reassurance of the continuity of life and man's essential nature despite external change. *Lark Rise to Candleford* is above all an affirmative work, offering a very positive view of the human condition, faith in the resilience of the human spirit and a belief in abiding human values.

Setting

Geographical

The trilogy is firmly based in the area where Flora Thompson spent her childhood (see the map at the front of this Study Aid). The hamlet of 'Lark Rise' is Juniper Hill, Lark Rise being the name of the large field by the cottage where the 'end house' family lived. 'Fordlow' is Cottisford, the nearby village. 'Candleford' is drawn from memories of Banbury, Bicester and Buckingham, mostly Buckingham since that is where the family went the first Sunday morning when they hired the pony-cart. The market town where the father worked is Brackley. The post office with attached forge described in *Over to Candleford* and *Candleford Green* can be found in Fringford, though Margaret Lane quotes a letter from Flora Thompson, in which she said that she had written more freely in those books than in *Lark Rise*, and did not describe any place exactly as it existed except the post office–forge and Shelswell Park, (the home of 'Sir Timothy' in *Purely for Pleasure*).

Actual place-names are used to reinforce the wider context of the Midlands location – Oxford, where her father once lived, is nineteen miles away according to the milestone on the children's favourite walk (2,33). One of the boys from the hamlet became a policeman at Birmingham (12,193); and Queenie sighs for the days when she used to sell her lace at Banbury Fair – now the rage is all for lace from Nottingham (5,84). There are many local details that can be traced with the aid of an Ordnance Survey map: for example, Mrs Herring refers to Tusmore House (20,296), which is south of Juniper Hill, off the A43 on the right from the Oxford approach; and Deddington, celebrated in song at the inn, is a nearby village (4,72).

Should a reader of the trilogy visit the area, he would experience great pleasure through an instant recognition of places, so detailed and exact are Flora Thompson's descriptions. Also striking is the fact that, to a visitor at any rate, scarcely anything seems to have changed since Flora Thompson was born there. The hamlet retains its basic shape, a huddle of houses first glimpsed from the

A43 with the white-painted 'end house' set on the very outskirts, turning its back on the rest. The approach is by a narrow track, as in the book, and a deeply rutted lane surrounds the whole. Certain buildings are easy to pick out immediately – the inn ('The Fox'), and 'Queen's Cottage', now occupied by the kindly Moreton family whose garden, where Queenie once kept the beehives, runs parallel to that of the end house, now half its former size and renamed 'Lark Rise Cottage'. And the road to Cottisford is indeed long and straight (11,173), and must have seemed never-ending to a small child walking to school.

The village itself has developed little since Flora Thompson wrote about it (3,47–8). The church is beautifully maintained: from the seat which the end house children occupied can be seen the line of trees and the gateway, a scene they enjoyed watching in summer (14,211); and on the wall above is the brass plate listing the names of those who died in the First World War: two columns of five names, with 'E. Timms' etched on a separate line below (15,247).

Flora Thompson makes these places live not only by her almost photographic reproduction of them in prose, but also by setting them against a vividly realized background of the English countryside with all its changing moods and seasons. We are always aware of the landscape and the weather, the varying colour of the fields from brown clay to green, then to the dark gold of late summer. Scenes which stay in the mind are: the frosty winter mornings, when farm boys had to be hauled out of their beds to force on shrunken boots hardened by the night's drying (3,48); Queenie dozing in the sunshine, waiting for her bees to swarm (5,82); Laura as a very small child in a field of daisies in the springtime (17,271); the autumn, when the harvest ripened, described in Chapter 15 and on Laura's return to Candleford (28,373); and, finally, the snow scene that greeted Laura on her first morning as postwoman (38,506).

The cumulative effect of the realism of the geographical setting, reinforced by a regional speech rich in proverbs and dialect terms, is to make this record of country life wholly credible to the reader. We accept the truth of Flora Thompson's memories more willingly because her people move and live in an authentic setting.

The remoteness of the location gives validity to her description of the self-contained world that developed there.

Historical

Lark Rise is set in the 1880s, *Over to Candleford* in the mid 1880s to early 1890s, and *Candleford Green* in the 1890s. These memories of Flora Thompson's early life are seen against a background of verifiable historical events. Sometimes she herself provides the dating, as for the General Election of 1886 (14,212) or the Queen's Jubilee of 1887 (15,239). More often references are worked into the plot seemingly as incidentals, thus cleverly managing to convey the sense of time passing, without constantly referring to the date. For instance, at the beginning of *Lark Rise* when Laura was very small, the newspaper cuttings decorating the walls of the euphemistically named 'little house' in the garden, all depicted disasters of the early 'eighties (1,23); the quarrel that arose between her father and Uncle James Dowland on the morning of the first visit to Candleford was over the question of Home Rule for Ireland, a topic that divided political opinion in the mid-eighties (21, 309–10). And the Oscar Wilde trial – which scandalized the village of Candleford Green, with unpleasant repercussions for the ex-Army pensioners Ben and Tom, who lived together (37,498) – took place in 1895. In this way the book is crowded with references to contemporary political and historical events, also with allusions to popular personalities, literature, and songs.

We are constantly aware of an individual life being passed in a particular historical context. This is important because, although the country was at peace and Queen Victoria's long reign gave the impression of domestic tranquillity, this was a period of far-reaching social and political change, themes that are reflected throughout the trilogy. In the historical setting, Flora Thompson seeks to establish the sense of an era poised midway between an old way of life and a new. On the one hand there is the old rural system, primarily feudal; on the other, the social and political reforms that paved the way for a different kind of society.

Early on in *Lark Rise to Candleford* Flora Thompson outlines the effects the Enclosure movement had on the area she is describing. Enclosing was a process that had begun in Tudor times, long before the Industrial Revolution. It was a means by which landowners were legally allowed to take over common land (used for the communal grazing of cattle, livestock and geese, and for gathering wood for fuel) and to add it to their own property – ostensibly to increase crop production – in return for cash or small plots of land for cottagers. From its earliest days, this produced strongly emotional reactions from writers, because of its overtones of the economic exploitation and dispossession of the peasantry. (The reaction of the latter is well known!) Towards the end of the eighteenth century Pitt had given considerable impetus to the Enclosure movement, as part of the overall policy of meeting demands for bread from the rapidly growing industrial areas. A local guide-book, *Cottisford and its Church* (still obtainable there), records how, as a result of the enclosing of Cottisford Heath into farms by an Act of Parliament in 1854, Juniper Hill grew from a few scattered cottages in the early part of the nineteenth century to the hamlet described by Flora Thompson.

Several squatters and smallholders, dispossessed by the enclosure, were allowed to rebuild at Juniper. In the opening chapter of *Lark Rise*, the houses occupied by the descendants of the original squatters are listed (1,18); and in Chapter 5 is given the history of Old Sally and Master Ashley, both of whom had inherited land. Succeeding generations in the hamlet did not possess the means to be independent in the style of Old Sally and her husband, Dick: they were all wage-earners living in rented cottages and (apart from Laura's father) employed by the farmer who lived at Cottisford and who – on behalf of an absentee landowner – farmed what had formerly been the Heath.

Lacking land and property, and being tied to a low wage, the men of Lark Rise greatly valued their newly acquired power to vote (4,65). In 1884 Gladstone had passed the Third Reform Act, which extended the franchise to some two million agricultural workers. Most of them exercised the vote in their class interests, feeling that the party of Gladstone, the Liberal Party, was the one for them. In the trilogy, the Conservative Party is always identified with the gentry and other authoritarian figures.

The other Act with importance in terms of the trilogy's historical setting was Forster's Education Act, passed in 1870, in which education was recognized as a public service. School attendance became compulsory in 1880, and children were legally obliged to stay at school until the age of ten. There was no minimum age of entry – Mrs Arless in fact sent her children at three (6,112). School Boards were set up to ensure that there was adequate provision for education in each area and to provide committees that could enforce attendance by law. How dreaded a figure the School Attendance Officer was locally is stressed by Flora Thompson in the opening chapters of *Lark Rise*.

Grants were awarded to individual schools on the basis of the numbers that attended, and on the percentage of pupils who passed the yearly tests, known as the examination of Standards. These ranged from Standards 1 to 6, and each Standard had to be passed before the next could be attempted. The examinations were carried out by Inspectors, who had almost absolute power. Mary Sturt, in *The Education of the People*, writes that it was 1890 before the teachers had any means of redress against unfair inspection. Many inspectors abused their powers, and became really hated during the 'eighties. This links interestingly with Flora Thompson's account in Chapter 12. Finally, though no child could legally leave school before the age of ten, the individual School Attendance Committees set up throughout the country often framed different by-laws governing attendance and exemption, linked with the passing of Standards. Clearly at Fordlow (Cottisford), children had to stay at school until they passed Standard 4 or reached their eleventh birthday, whichever came first (11,182; 28,376–7). They could stay longer, as Laura did, if their parents were willing to forgo their earning power; obviously many parents were not so willing, as her only companion during the two years she was in Standard 5 was her friend Emily Rose, significantly an only child (11,184, and more fully in Chapter 28).

Social

In discussing her lack of political stance in later life, (in the third part of the trilogy, *Candleford Green*), Flora Thompson writes of Laura that, although she had been brought up by her father in the Liberal tradition and 'loved the Liberals, and afterwards the Socialists for their efforts to improve the lot of the poor', yet 'in spite of her early training, the inborn cast of her mind, with its love of the past and of the English countryside, often drew her in the opposite direction' (35,467). Her presentation of the social setting, and social change, frequently echoes this essential ambiguity in her attitude. There is social satire in many of her portraits, and criticism of social injustices (such as the low pay of the farm labourers), but there is at the same time a basic approval of the past and the old ways. As with the historical setting, her view encompasses the old and the new. Though class barriers remained fairly rigid for a long time after this period, the attitudes of individual characters are used to reinforce the sense of a social scene slowly changing, (as will be shown in the section on *Characters*).

Flora Thompson distinguishes between the social structure found in hamlet, town and village, so they are described separately here.

Hamlet

In so far as there was a social élite in the hamlet, the end house family clearly belonged to it, together with the family at the inn and Old Sally, who also had slightly more means than the rest. Basically, though, there was only one class of people: they all did the same work for the same wage and so were equals in poverty. Life was hard for everybody, and all had an unending struggle to make ends meet. Though the cottages they lived in were rented for one or two shillings a week from small tradesmen in the market town, the great attraction of living at Juniper was that the cottages were 'free'. Farm labourers often had the choice of living on the land of their employers, perhaps rent-free or for a few pence a week, but in a 'tied' cottage – meaning that the house went with the job. The hamlet housed a poor but independent-minded community, who stayed in bed on Sunday mornings if they felt like it and voted as they pleased.

They might look to the Rectory for a pair of boots on occasion, but largely they worked on a democratic basis of relying on one another in times of trouble, illness or childbirth, on the understanding that this help would be returned when necessary. Attractive though her portrait of neighbourly behaviour is, Flora Thompson makes clear it had its limits. Borrowers were regarded as a permanent nuisance and when the public wells dried up in summer, those who owned private ones shut them up and 'disregarded all hints' (1,22–3). It is important to note that the 'bettermost' people who they knew, the doctor, the Rector, the Squire and his mother, all lived elsewhere than the hamlet and only called as visitors, who could even be kept waiting on the doorstep if need be, as poor Miss Ellison, the Rector's daughter, often was. Consequently, they felt free to take their 'social superiors' very much as they found them, and often in a far from deferential spirit, as described later under Neighbours in our section on *Characters*.

Town

Mrs Herring, the landlady from Candleford, made clear on her visit to Lark Rise that social life in the town differed greatly from that in the hamlet – a concept Laura found hard to grasp. Rachel's friendly enquiries were dismissed by Mrs Herring as impertinence of a kind she would not have to put up with in Candleford, for *there* poor people kept to their part of the town and she kept to hers (20,298–9). But when the end house family went 'over to Candleford' to visit their relatives, they did not in fact go to visit 'poor people' of the social class despised by Mrs Herring: both Candleford uncles were self-employed men with thriving businesses, one being a builder, the other a shoemaker. Uncle James Dowland was much richer than Uncle Tom, but both families kept house in a style far beyond the means of anybody in Lark Rise. Laura, when she later spent the summer holidays in Candleford, stayed with Aunt Ann and Uncle Tom, with occasional visits across the town to the Dowlands.

Laura did not personally experience the poorer side of town life, but there are enough details in the text to make clear her awareness that contrasts existed, side by side, in a way that they did not in Lark Rise. For instance, on the first visit, when the children walked across the town with their mother, Laura commented on the slums they passed and was hastily silenced. The less fortunate had to rely almost totally on the charitable feelings of the more well-to-do. For example, her Aunt Ann employed a workhouse orphan Benny to do odd jobs, and at Aunt Edith's, Laura made the acquaintance of the simple-minded Bertha, mother of an illegitimate child. When she spent days in the workshop with Uncle Tom she heard stories of deprivation and hardship from the young doctor who was fond of visiting him (27,356). Thus, the dichotomy in the social setting of Candleford opened Laura's eyes to the economic realities of a wider world.

Village

In the world of Candleford Green, Flora Thompson offers a conventional picture of village life, familiar from the writings of others: for example, Miss Mitford's *Our Village* and Mrs Gaskell's *Cranford*. Candleford Green was built quite literally round a central green, with shops and businesses interspersed among private houses and cottages. The daily contact of the various classes – gentry, professionals, tradesmen and labourers – meant that modes of social behaviour were on the whole rigidly adhered to. The social hierarchy was clearly defined, and people talked proudly of knowing their place and keeping to it (32,417).

In times of sickness and hardship the gentry, the Rectory and the better-off such as Miss Lane, were looked to for help; and any assistance given was received gratefully, with no sense of awkwardness on either side. This was very different from the hamlet attitude to charity and patronage: indeed, Miss Ellison's 'Box' which she lent for confinements was invariably taken for granted, so much so that one woman went as far as tearing off some of the lace she did not like (8,133–4), and Mrs Bracewell was advised by some of the women (behind her back) to 'stay at home and see that her own tea-caddy's kept locked up, not come nosing round here axin' how many spoonsful we puts in ours' (12,195). Laura was in a fairly privileged position in this small world, as personal friend and assistant to Miss Lane (see *Characters*).

Cultural

In the trilogy, emphasis is placed on the fact that, though the age of the wage-earner had arrived, the people in the rural communities here described were still self-supporting and self-sufficient in many ways. They made their own bread (from 'leazings', which they gathered in family groups at Lark Rise); brewed wines and beers; and preserved jams and jellies. Vegetables were all home grown and pigs and poultry were kept, though the old communal grazing rights had been lost. Life was still tied to the rhythms of the year and the land, in a celebratory way handed down through centuries of tradition. Particularly striking are the descriptions of May Day and Harvest Home in *Lark Rise*, and Miss Lane's own version of a harvest-home supper in *Candleford Green*. As with the dancing and rhyming games in the evenings, and the singing at the inn, these were essentially communal activities – originating from the culture of the people themselves and characteristically vigorous and lively. There is a nice moment on the May Day walk when the Lark Rise–Fordlow faction meet a rival group from a nearby village on the road: their recorded reactions do not suggest that such activities in any way heightened their sensibilities (13, 206–7)!

Life was still lived at a leisurely pace; there was no traffic on the roads and people walked the distance between hamlet and market town as a matter of course. Hiring a pony-cart was for special occasions only. But, as in the historical and social settings, Flora Thompson's method is to show how the old and the new slowly mingled. The songs sung at the inn and at the school concerts began to include some from the contemporary music-hall; factory-produced furniture was often preferred to the craftsman-made; newspapers replaced the Bible as the basic written authority; and bicycles appeared in considerable numbers. The actual places were altering – for instance, the carpentry business run by the three Williams made way for a builder's showroom – and suburban growth from Candleford straggled out to meet Candleford Green.

At the end of *Candleford Green*, Flora Thompson is outspokenly critical about the cultural changes that took place at the end of the century. She provides a heavily satirical portrait of the essential sterility of the lifestyle she saw evolving in a household such as the Greens (Chapter 39). Her concluding remarks indicate that she believed the society replacing the old way of life, while materially improved, was spiritually impoverished. She adds that the new creed was that of 'keeping up appearances', and in so doing people were neglecting much that had created the quality of rural life (pp.535–6). This concluding diatribe could possibly be viewed as a last-minute lack of artistic confidence in the author – a failure to trust the tale to have conveyed imaginatively to the reader a sufficient sense of what had been lost.

Themes

H. J. Massingham (1888–1952), author of the Introduction which prefaced the 1945 edition of the trilogy, and which now prefaces the Penguin Modern Classics edition, was all his life a passionate advocate of the spiritual value of a life lived close to the land, a belief expressed in works such as *The Faith of a Fieldsman* and *A Countryman's Journal.* His generous praise of Flora Thompson's trilogy emphasizes that in *Lark Rise to Candleford* he found a view of social history (of which he approved) given literary expression of a high order. Massingham introduces *Lark Rise to Candleford* as essentially 'the story of the irreparable calamity of the English fields' (Introduction, p.10); an obliquely presented version of the 'great tragic epic', defined as the demolition of 'the structure and the pattern of country life' by the Industrial Revolution and the Enclosures (p.14). Old Sally, Queenie, and Uncle Tom are cited as the central pivot of the work, the best of an 'Old England' that had practically vanished by the period when the trilogy begins. His strong feelings of distaste for the subsequent urban and industrial age are shared by many 20th-century writers, among them the late Dr F. R. Leavis. H. J. Massingham's Introduction apparently met with Flora Thompson's approval (see *Purely for Pleasure*), for she had worked hard throughout the trilogy to make clear that she was writing with a didactic purpose (see the sections on *Approach* and *Cultural Setting*).

In his well-known essay on 'The Spirit of Place', in *Studies in Classic American Literature* (Penguin). D. H. Lawrence wrote: 'The artist usually sets out – or used to – to point a moral and adorn a tale. The tale, however, points the other way, as a rule. Two blankly opposing morals, the artist's and the tale's. Never trust the artist. Trust the tale. The proper function of a critic is to save the tale from the artist who created it.' If the reader follows Lawrence's advice and trusts the tale, often the heartfelt cry which emanates from the book seems to be not only 'People were happier then', but '*I* was happier then'. For the strong sense of nostalgia is expressed not only in the objective terms of social record, it is made intensely personal by the autobiographical element of the trilogy.

Flora Thompson writes totally without self-pity, and the fact that she is recalling with such affection family and friends who are dead, makes this particularly painful reading. Powerfully conveyed beneath the surface pleasures of the pastoral scene of a 'better age' is the feeling of underlying regret for the loss of innocence, for the fading of the childish vision that had seen Lark Rise, not as a poor hamlet, but as a beautiful place surrounded by flowers and fields, and peopled with endlessly entertaining, larger-than-life grown-ups who could cope with anything. Like the other girls of her social class who left at an early age to go into service, when she left Lark Rise, she left behind her childhood status. *Lark Rise to Candleford* is a book about growing up and going away – it tells of the importance of 'roots' as a life-long point of reference in the search of the individual for personal values in a changing world.

The social and personal nostalgia in the trilogy is not in itself without ambiguity, for *Lark Rise to Candleford* has the complexity of vision that characterizes all truly creative work. In the adaptation from the trilogy for the stage production, Keith Dewhurst emphasized not only the quality of life in the rural past, but also the social injustice and exploitation that were also features of that time, an approach which was theatrically very effective. Similarly the personal nostalgia is made more poignant by the fact that Flora Thompson never felt her family really belonged to the hamlet – the theme of the outsider is a recurrent one in the trilogy – and reference is made in the section on *Characters* to the way in which the end house family were set apart in Lark Rise, in varying degrees as individuals, as their house was physically set apart. But, as she portrays herself in Laura, she was more than a social outsider, she was an outsider by virtue of her nature and her gifts. The portrait of Laura offers comment on the isolated position of the artist in society, for her position in town or village is the same: that of the eternal observer.

From her experiences in these different contexts, Flora Thompson's awareness of class-consciousness emerged. This theme is presented often in terms of the individuals she met, and frequently accompanied by satire and symbolic juxtaposition of opposing viewpoints (see the section on *Characters*). As children, Laura and Edmund did not realize 'when their mother told them that the greatest mistake in life is to be born poor . . . that they themselves had made that initial blunder' (16,249). To some extent the narrative line traces their growing comprehension of this fact; and that the wonderful world of Lark Rise came very low on the social scale in a world where they would be judged in social terms. The first clues came through their experience of education; their father did not want them to go to the National school; their Aunt made clear there would be no Oxford and Cambridge for Edmund; Miss Holmes's teaching was aimed at indoctrinating them into acceptance of their lowly place, and the rector reinforced this theme in his scripture lessons and at church. Though Miss Shepherd encouraged free-thinking, in practice she was a snob and a would-be social climber.

Laura overheard talk in the hamlet about former times and the dispossession of the peasantry; and social attitudes as they existed are recorded (Chapters 14 and 19). Mrs Herring's use of the word 'civilized' puzzled her, and Candleford widened her view of the world and what the possession of money meant. Her cousins demonstrated different attitudes to experience because of their wider education, at school and at home. At Candleford Green, as at Candleford, her status was fairly privileged and the ambiguity of her position was underlined by her uneasiness with the new-found friends who talked of cottage people in a way that grated, also her failure to understand Mrs Green's use of the word 'common' is a social sense. Constantly, the reader is made aware of social change, of old attitudes being questioned and barriers broken.

This theme is linked with Laura's increasing awareness of role-conditioning – she was at a disadvantage in the world's eyes, not only by birth but by sex. Note that it is the men of Lark Rise who have the vote and the money for the evening drink, and the boys who are favoured by their mothers though the girls make the sacrifices, and this state of affairs does not go uncommented upon.

Though Flora Thompson differs strikingly from D. H. Lawrence in her reluctance to deal with the feelings of the characters she portrays, there is, at the same time, much of Lawrence's concept of the 'life-force' in her trilogy. This is seen in her support of the natural as opposed to the artificial; her trust in the emotional, not the intellectual, response; and is given fullest expression in her belief in Nature as a regenerative and healing force (28,384). This positive feeling is strengthened by its reverse side: her horror of death and at the sight of dead things. This is seen not only in relation to the pig, but whenever she has come across death, as a child or adolescent (for example, 34,452). Finally, the all-embracing range of Flora Thompson's portrayal of people as individuals – as real today as when she knew them – adds to the feeling of life as a continuous process, of the human spirit rising phoenix-like, despite external change. It is this that makes the trilogy such an affirmative and lastingly relevant work.

Structure

The literary genre to which *Lark Rise to Candleford* belongs, as part-record and part-autobiography, has been outlined in the section on *Approach*. Structurally, the trilogy rests on a juxtaposition of past and present, and a dual time-scheme is operated. For the most part, it is a careful reconstruction of the period of Flora Thompson's youth in the 'eighties and 'nineties, as seen through the eyes of the child Laura, the author's name for herself. But this illusion of a reconstituted world is frequently dispelled by the voice of Flora Thompson, the author, speaking directly to the reader; and we are brought out of the world of the past into that of the 1930s and early 1940s. This device is frequently found in 19th-century novels, and is known as authorial intervention. It is often linked, as in this case, to an overall didactic purpose. Here, the reader's attention is drawn frequently to the inadequacies of the modern world – in its basic quality (3,64), and in its trivia. (She complains at one point – 7,121 – that even modern tomatoes are inferior!) Sometimes authorial intervention is used to tell the reader what happened to a character in later life. In this way it is possible to piece together the history of the end house family and some of their friends from Candleford Green.

The trilogy was published as three separate books, the last two being written in response to public demand (see the section *The author and her work*). Flora Thompson is careful to unify the three into an artistic whole. The most obvious structural link is the character of the narrator Laura, for each book carries her history a little further. In her own person she unites hamlet, town and village, since part of her life is passed in each of these places. It is important to note that *Laura is a child*, because this inevitably limits the range of her vision and at the same time accounts for the air of innocence and freshness, of things newly seen, that characterizes the approach. There is, for example, no overt sense of sexuality, despite the chapters on 'The Box' and 'Men Afield' (compare the account of village life in the nineteenth century in a work such as Émile Zola's *Germinal*). Margaret Lane mentions in passing, in her *Purely for Pleasure*, that several children in the Timms family died young (as was common in large Victorian families), but there is no reference to child death in *Lark Rise to Candleford*. Always in the period recalled there was someone else who made the decisions and took the responsibility – parents, kind aunts and uncles, a family friend – and this is all part of the remembrance of a golden age of youth.

Each book differs somewhat in character. *Lark Rise* is the longest and the most schematic. The record predominates over the autobiographical element, and the book is really a series of beautifully organized essays on distinct topics – religion, education, domestic arrangements and so on – held together by the character of Laura, and by the firm nature of the subject: the hamlet of Lark Rise. It is interesting that the title of the second book is not 'Candleford' but *Over to Candleford*, and because the book encompasses town and hamlet as its subject a rather looser structure evolves. Its early chapters elaborate on information already given (in *Lark Rise*, Chapters 15 and 16), about the inhabitants of the hamlet generally; (Chapters 17 and 18), and about the end house specifically. The idea of going to Candleford to see the richer relatives is introduced in the opening sentence of the second book and it acts as a refrain, which makes for a separate internal structure of this part of the trilogy. Chapter 20 introduces Mrs Herring, the landlady from Candleford, which brings the town to the forefront of the narrative and prepares the way for the two following chapters, which are set there. These two are held together by juxtaposition as the two families of relatives are strikingly contrasted. The policy of elaboration of basic information given in *Lark Rise* continues in those remaining parts of the second book that are set in the hamlet; and the reader is given a much more personal account of how Laura coped with school and home. *Over to Candleford* ends with Laura leaving the village to take up her post as assistant to Miss Lane at Candleford Green which Laura had visited earlier (see Chapter 27).

Over to Candleford is different from *Lark Rise* in that the overall structure is more varied in character, and the emphasis moves from record to autobiography. *Candleford Green* is closer to *Lark Rise* in that the basic subject is a single one – the village of

Candleford Green – with Laura making only one visit to the hamlet. Aspects of village life are covered in the same orderly way that is familiar from the structure of *Lark Rise.* But the story line is even more apparent than in *Over to Candleford*, and *Candleford Green* is closer to an autobiographical novel as such than either of the previous two. *Lark Rise to Candleford* is an interesting example of a work in which a character begins to take over in a way almost contrary to the author's avowed intentions. As the trilogy gathers force, Flora Thompson intervenes less frequently in her didactic role – as she gains confidence she often lets the narrative speak more directly to the reader.

Themes and certain characters (particularly the end house family) recur throughout the trilogy and strengthen the unity of the whole. Also, Laura has a substitute mother-figure in Aunt Ann (*Over to Candleford*) and in Miss Lane (*Candleford Green*). Finally, Flora Thompson illustrates her dramatic skill in structure as well as in characterization, in that each part of the trilogy ends almost like an Act in a traditionally structured play, with a strong curtain line – Edmund's death at the end of *Lark Rise*, Laura's departure to *Candleford Green* at the end of the second book, and, at the end of *Candleford Green*, her exit from the 'stage' where the trilogy has been set.

Style

In *Lark Rise to Candleford* Flora Thompson slowly and lovingly builds up a whole world by means of careful presentation of detail. She had originally attracted the attention of the Oxford University Press because of her ability as an *essayist*, a skill much in evidence in the trilogy. She writes in a clear, unpretentious style, and each chapter has its own internal structure and organization, as well as being an intrinsic part of the overall vision. The opening lines of the chapters are particularly arresting, and designed to capture the reader's interest anew. The trilogy is enriched throughout by the *use of direct speech*, often proverbial or in dialect, which brings the record to life in human terms; for example, Mrs Herring was not just mean, 'She wer' that near she 'udn't give away enough to make a pair of leggings for a skylark' (17,263).

When Flora Thompson feels the use of local idiom might cause difficulty for the reader she often includes her own *editorial explanations*, as in the record of the field-names (3,52), and of the term 'Bavour' (p.54). This conscientious approach is evident throughout the trilogy, and helps to make the record of life in the past so remarkable. Linked with this is her poet's gift for *descriptive* writing, for recreating a scene in terms of sight, sound and smell. Particularly notable is the pig-killing near the opening of the trilogy (1,26). This degree of vivid realism is partly achieved by the exactness of her recall of all the small details, and is evident in many less dramatic passages – for instance, in the scene-setting of a typical Sunday morning in Church (14,211), or in domestic detail, such as the housewife blowing on her fingers as she unwraps the hot roly-poly (10,171). There are countless examples of this kind of attention to the minutiae of everyday experience. She often uses *homely or natural similes* – the end house children liked the untarred road surface, and would 'splash up the thin, pale mud, *like uncooked batter*' (2,34); Gertie's husband, in his finery, wore a chrysanthemum '*as big as a pancake*' (19,286); and, contrasting the life of the country rich and poor, 'The gentry flitted across the scene *like kingfishers crossing a flock of hedgerow sparrows*' (16,253).

Flora Thompson's poetic gifts are given more direct expression in her *natural descriptions* – see the section on *Setting* (*Geographical*). There is an almost Wordsworthian belief in the healing effects of natural scenes, and this apprehension is presented symbolically at the end of Chapter 28. Like Wordsworth, she is particularly fine at conveying the silence of the countryside. *Symbolism* is used occasionally in the trilogy to reinforce a point about a theme or character – for example, the end house, Miss Lane's clocks, or the dead pig in the pantry.

Finally, the outstandingly attractive feature of Flora Thompson's style is *her sense of humour and irony*, which makes the country scene she portrays so vastly entertaining.

Snatches of neighbours' conversation throughout add to the comic effectiveness of the whole, though in this respect the inhabitants of Lark Rise upstage everybody else in the book. Often she sees situations as essentially comic; for instance, as Mrs Herring sips tea genteelly, her hat is slipping and her husband is busy letting the side down by eating all the cakes and dipping the lettuce straight into the salt-cellar (Chapter 20). This illustrates one of Flora Thompson's favourite techniques – she loves to highlight the difference between pretension and fact, illusion and reality. There are many examples of this, and there are often class overtones too: lower-middle-class morality and attitudes being set against a more down-to-earth working-class actuality. Uncle James Dowland teaches the poor children the temperance song, plaintively beseeching their fathers to forbear drink and 'come home', when the fathers are already at home – only being able to afford a modest half-pint – and the singers will be the ones in trouble for being out late (21,307).

The author is also fond of letting people condemn themselves; she merely records their remarks, without comment. Philip White comes in for such treatment in Chapter 38; again, her 'straight' reporting of her mother's remarks on Mrs Braddon and Shakespeare is masterly (2,38). Sometimes she lets people says things to their disadvantage, then pretends, innocently, to agree – a favourite Chaucerian device. After recording that a man in Candleford Green said it would break his heart to see his wife on a bicycle, she slyly adds that those acquainted with his wife's figure thought this reasonable (35,477). Another recurrent source of humour throughout is at her own expense: she is fond of including the unflattering comments, intended to be helpful, which all and sundry make on her appearance.

A final illustration of Flora Thompson's general excellence as a writer lies in the fact that she knows exactly how to place a verb or adjective for maximum effect: for example, to highlight a discrepancy between word and deed. At the 'Wagon and Horses', Sam voices his radical opinions loudly but waves his glass aloft 'very *carefully*, for every drop was precious' (4,66). There is a similar irony in the portrait of her friends in their early twenties demonstrating their avant-garde approach by walking hatless over Hindhead at night in a gale, '*bawling*' poetry above the storm (28,379). At the end of *Lark Rise* the author catches up a word used earlier in a lighter context, and uses it with deadly effect in a more sombre setting – for in the First World War the men from Lark Rise did not 'flinch'; consequently, many, including Edmund, did not come back.

Characters

Flora Thompson later described the characterization of *Lark Rise* as pure record – the people all existed, there was no invention – whereas in *Over to Candleford* and *Candleford Green* she often drew on several sources in depicting a person, as she had done in depicting a place (*Purely for Pleasure*). But the trilogy is the work of an imaginative writer of considerable strength, and how far any such work involving creative processes can ever be an act of total recall is a matter for debate. There always seems to be a point where realism takes over from reality, art from life. Laurie Lee acknowledged this difficulty more openly in his childhood reminiscences of rural life described in *Cider with Rosie*. For one thing the view we are given of the people who inhabit her world is a subjective one, whether recorded through the child Laura or in the author's own voice. Also important is the fact that all the characters are observed from the outside. They are vividly captured in terms of appearance, behaviour and speech. Sometimes we are told what their neighbours thought of them as well, but we are not told how they think or behave when by themselves. Basically, Flora Thompson is concerned with the public face, not with the private man or woman.

Throughout the trilogy, though the author is clearly using a novelist's skill in choosing anecdotes, incidents and conversation to present (and perhaps embellish) her characters, there is, apart from the character of Laura, no real sense of people changing and developing through interaction and experience, as we might expect in a novel. They come to us fully developed, and the book acts almost as a stage on which they pass continually before us, gaining their vitality from the shrewdness of their creator's observation and graphic descriptions. Some are presented as vivid thumbnail sketches: for instance, the gypsy-like Lily, 'big and strong and clumsy as a carthorse' (3,58); or Mrs Gubbins, the bad-tempered postwoman at Candleford Green. Others are described at greater length, as are many of the friends and neighbours in hamlet, village and town: for example, Mrs Herring; Bertha, the maid at the Dowlands; or Willy at Candleford Green. However, they usually put in only one or two appearances and then are seen no more.

A few characters recur throughout, notably Laura's family, who are described in a wider variety of contexts. These are full character portraits, but again the reader is kept at arm's length. We are given more external details of the end house family as the trilogy progresses, but there is no attempt to portray the family relationships in all their complexity. Take, for example, the relationship between the parents: hints are dropped in *Lark Rise* about their marital tensions, and these are enlarged upon in *Over to Candleford.* From the start the mother has badly miscalculated the depth of her husband's radical feelings. She has little patience with his lack of social ambition, or what she regards as his peculiar ideas on the brotherhood of man (7,125) – having married him thinking he was a promising young man from Oxford! She frequently discusses her unhappiness with her father in Laura's hearing, and, particularly after her husband turns increasingly to drink, makes disparaging remarks about people who 'ought to be ashamed of themselves for coming down in the world' (18,274). She urges Edmund to think of becoming a carpenter, because 'it was cleaner work than that of a mason and carpenters did not drink in public-houses as masons did, and people respected them more' (p.278). But the tone of these remarks indicates that Flora Thompson does not intend us to take them too seriously.

To illustrate this point by extreme contrast, consider how differently the theme of a drunken father and a socially ambitious mother is explored in the characterization of D. H. Lawrence's *Sons and Lovers*, based on his memories of working-class life; or how L. P. Hartley presents a close brother-sister relationship in *The Shrimp and the Anemone*. Both these writers would seem to exemplify, in the intensity of the relationships they portray, the kind of emotional depths Flora Thompson was most anxious to avoid in writing about herself – as she frequently tells us by means of authorial intervention (2,46; 35,475).

Certainly, in *Lark Rise to Candleford*, the author wishes her readers to keep their distance. She seems happiest when viewing her people as social characters on whom she can, directly or indirectly, make a moral comment as they wend their way through what is predominantly a comic scene. Her sharp eye for human frailty has been commented on in the section on *Style*; and, on one level, her book reads like a comedy of manners. She has the dramatist's gift for revealing character in the way people look, behave and, most of all, speak. Often the speech recorded allows full play to her sense of the ironic; but some of the exchanges show her as masterly in the art of comic dialogue (see particularly Chapter 20). This gift for being able to make people talk convincingly in character, combined with her easy command of vernacular speech, leads to some of the trilogy's most effective moments (see Queenie's comments on the milk intended for her pig, 1,31). But though she is always ready to be entertained by her fellow men, and entertain us in turn, she is at the same time enormously sympathetic in her approach. She interprets people's motives generously, and usually gives them the benefit of the doubt when these motives seem mixed (see, for example, 21,308).

Flora Thompson is not, however, totally impartial in her recollections, and some people are given a more satirical treatment than others. She has a fondness for independent characters who keep themselves to themselves – for example, Old Sally, Queenie and Miss Lane and for the solitary. Note, in this context, the similarity between Mrs Merton (Chapter 19) and Mrs Macey, the younger postwoman at Candleford Green whom Laura eventually replaces. She loves the good: her grandfather or old Mr Marley, the curate, both of whom delight in giving, and the kindly; her Uncle Tom, Sir Timothy of Candleford Green, and Matthew, who manages the forge there. Flora Thompson is basically on the side of the life-enhancers, particularly those with a strong appetite for life.

Far from perfect, but very good fun, are the irrepressible Rachel and the exuberant Mrs Arless, who devotes herself with as much energy to her beer-drinking as to defending her way of life regularly at the County Court, where her creditors were the ones who were invariably discomfited. The people she is rather harsher on are the non-contributors to life those, who, through vanity or general narrowness of outlook, devote themselves entirely to their own small, selfish concerns, oblivious of the needs and feelings of others. In this group can be included the pretty, empty-headed women such as her grandmother, who sits reading novelettes among her feather cushions while her husband is dying, slowly and painfully, in the room above (5,94); Gertie, the simpering, fading beauty of Lark Rise (Chapter 19), who also prefers to live by illusion rather than reality, endlessly romanticizing about her past conquests and ignoring her doting husband; and Mrs Green, from the new villas outside Candleford Green, fanatically cleaning an already spotless house, and despising her common neighbours (Chapter 39).

It is no coincidence that Philip White, Laura's would-be suitor, is also vain and self-preoccupied (assuring Laura that all in his family are good-looking), as well as being pompous, boring and totally smug (38,517–22). The moral criticism is often linked with social satire, as in the case of Mrs Green, but also in the portrayal of the Rector and his daughter, the farmer at Fordlow, and Mrs Bracewell, the Squire's mother. Some of the characters would seem to carry symbolic weight as well as their role as realistic characters (see the section on *Themes*, and the individual character studies which follow in this section).

The pitfall in this continuous presentation of character sketches, in a trilogy of such length, is that it could become monotonous, even glib. Sometimes it seems that Flora Thompson is in danger of exaggerating moral character to differentiate people – she does not physically distort, as Dickens often did, but she makes some characters entirely 'nice' (Mrs Beer, 33,441–3), or entirely 'nasty' (the Lark Rise postman, 6,101–2) in their very brief appearance. Also her favourite structure of three, used in describing the fieldwoman (Chapter 3) or the schoolmistresses (Chapter 11), becomes rather obtrusive after a time. On the whole, though, her people are endlessly engaging simply because she is able to communicate so well their original fascination for her. Only occasionally does her memory seem forced and her characters consciously 'quaint' – for example, the description of the elderly courting couple, Chokey and Bess of Lark Rise (Chapter 10), both obviously rather simple-minded, whose 'funny little wedding' and 'funny little house' we seem to be invited to laugh at in a spirit uncharacteristic of this author (p.169). Similarly, Chapter 26 in *Over to Candleford* entitled 'Uncle Tom's Queer Fish' describes the people who visited her uncle's workshop as 'oddities', in a curiously superior and unexpected way. Readers may well differ in interpretation of authorial attitudes – it is the sort of book where certain people become firm favourites. This is perhaps the most telling comment on Flora Thompson's characterization, for above all she is able to present characters who live on in our imagination and command our loyalties long after the book has been closed.

The end house family

Mother

Mother was there, Mother in her pretty maize-coloured gown with the rows and rows of narrow brown velvet sewn round the long skirt which stuck out like a bell, and her second-best hat with the honeysuckle (2,36–7).

This sentimental childhood view of pretty, wonderful Mother, always kind, always there and always right, is one which dominates the landscape of Laura and Edmund in their pre-school years. Flora Thompson's achievement in portraying her mother in the trilogy is in conveying how, as Laura grew up, her mother gradually became reduced in size (as in one sense, literally so, since she remains 'the pocket Venus' while her daughter towers above) until she became another person, still a remarkable woman, but a recognizable human being, not an idealization. It is a masterly portrait, combining both humour and affection, for Laura and her mother view life very differently, and many of the mother's sayings and aspirations are presented tongue-in-cheek, even while there is no question of her daughter's basic admiration.

Laura's mother has had a better education than many girls of her social class. She has been brought up in a cottage adjoining a churchyard in a neighbouring village, and the sister of the Rector has taken an interest in her as a child, teaching her singing and writing. Later she was a children's nurse at a local rectory before she married. She is at her best with small children, and knows instinctively how to make them feel secure. She orders their daily routine to a predictable pattern, and provides a stimulating environment including walks (Chapter 2), stories (Chapter 18), and what would now be called 'the opportunity for creative play' (17,264).

Finally, Laura's mother has an unquestioning belief in her own fitness for the job and is totally self-confident. She likes her children to be obedient and well-behaved, and has no hesitation in administering instant discipline to achieve this end, as when the children wake the baby doing the polka (12,200), or when Laura goes ice-skating without permission (23,326). She is unwavering in her standards, which again add to their feeling of general security when small. In some ways she always remains the professional nanny – passionately fond of the newest arrival but unable to relate so well to the demands of the older children. This causes problems for Laura in her teens (28,380).

She is practical in her role of mother, and also in the management of her home. We are told she has notions of 'seemliness' (28,379), which largely consist of keeping her house and children scrupulously clean, and providing a sensible diet – no small achievement on a weekly income of fifteen shillings, in a house with no running water. She is a clever needlewoman and often sits up half the night altering and adapting parcels of clothes sent by richer relatives (28,380). She shows practical kindness, offering nursing assistance or food to, for example the old Major (5,88–9), and to Mr Marley, whom she suspects of neglecting himself physically in the pursuit of more spiritual matters (14,227–8). Later, she helps people in the hamlet who have lost their pigs in the swine-fever epidemic (18,279).

She is able to adjust to circumstances: although, like her husband, she is an outsider to the hamlet, and her social attitudes are those of a villager, she is at the same time ready to fall in with some of the hamlet ways while the family lives there. She allows the children to play outside, against her husband's wishes, because she feels it will be better for them when they go to school if they have already mixed locally. She wants them to 'get on' in life, in the traditional ways open to the aspiring working class (2,42), and she distrusts intellectual interests as being 'clever' and an obstacle to such advancement (p.38). In the trilogy her essential conservatism of outlook is set against her husband's radical views, often for humorous effect, as in her reported reaction to his encounter with the some of the homeless poor (7,125).

Flora Thompson secures the reader's sympathy and respect for her mother in two ways. Firstly, though she stresses her extraordinary competence and organizational powers, she also shows her as being in some ways at a disadvantage. Her predicament is essentially that of an extremely conventional woman faced with an unconventional family; and, from a villager's point of view, equally unconventional neighbours. And this situation is recorded by the author with some degree of amusement. Though her chosen friends are rather genteel they have their shortcomings: at any moment Rachel is likely to drift in for a 'bit of a tell', followed by half the hamlet; and the mother's belief in social tact, in always doing and saying the 'right thing' and giving offence to nobody, is more of a hindrance than a help when trying to deal with barefaced cheek (see her ineffectual attempts at putting off the borrowers, (6,107–8).

Secondly, Flora Thompson makes clear from a variety of incidents that the mother is not perfect. Clearly she has been rather spoilt in early life as the pretty youngest child of a large family (one of her first actions on learning to talk was to insist that her two nieces, both older than herself, should address her as 'Aunt', 5,91). Her father has always doted on her, listened to her troubles and reproved his grandchildren if they caused her extra work. By temperament and upbringing, then, she very much likes getting her own way, and is invariably sure her way is right. Neither is she an impartial mother – we are told that on several occasions she prefers her sons to her daughters (2,44; 3,55; and 17,268).

Our final view of the mother (in terms of the chronological order of events), shows her as a woman both stoic and dignified, living alone in the end house after her husband has died and her children have left (2,42), with her wish for 'thirty shillings weekly, regularly paid', ironically fulfilled by the supplement from the Mother's Pension received for her dead son (18,276).

Father

Even in darkness his step could be distinguished, for it was lighter and sharper than that of the other men (17,262).

Flora Thompson's father is presented, through Laura's father, as an outsider to the hamlet, socially and temperamentally; and, more symbolically, as an outsider to the more positive aspects of life it represents. He has originally come to the area with a firm of builders engaged in the restoration of some of the churches in the countryside, met and married the children's mother, and settled in Lark Rise. His parents lived in Oxford when he was a small child, and three of his sisters are described in the trilogy. Since all three are relatively well-off, Laura's mother would seem to have some justification in purely social terms for her jibes about her husband having come down in the world. The father has worked in the market town (Brackley) for thirty-five years for a firm of builders (17,261). Although he never likes Lark Rise and makes no attempt to become a part of the hamlet, he never moves away and, it seems, dies there in the 1930s (2,42). He earns more than the other men in the hamlet, who are all farm workers; and he pays more in rent for what is effectively two cottages joined into one (p.263).

In her father Flora Thompson offers a moving portrait of a man in whom idealism has turned sour. In the outline of his life there are echoes of the tragic hero of Hardy's *Jude the Obscure*. He was extremely handsome and striking-looking as a young man (p.262), intellectually gifted and artistic (p.261). His high hopes of life are evident in the care he put into his work, his creativity in carving, and the romantic youthful marriage he made, for clearly it was an affair of the heart (18,272). In Chapter 17 of the trilogy, where Flora Thompson describes the father most fully, she contrasts this positive approach of youth symbolized by his quickness of mind and movement) with his character and appearance in old age: a broken man, apparently ruined by drink.

But in the course of the trilogy a fuller portrait of the father emerges, and it becomes increasingly clear that drink is the effect and not the cause of his decline. He is an intellectual caught in a basic dilemma: he despises the society he lives in, but also despises his own lowly position within it. He is totally unable to compromise, to accept his own human limitations, those of his fellow-men, or those of imperfect human institutions. Because he cannot accept reality he turns gradually from idealism to cynicism, and embarks upon a course of self-destruction. We are invited to feel pity at this waste of a human being, but not to blame.

The father is shown initially as a person to command our admiration, for he is a man of integrity. He is outspoken about his socialist politics, and he is also open about his agnosticism (14,228). That his attitudes are motivated by principles of a high order is indicated by his annoyance with one of the old Radical voters who accepted a free lift to the polling station from the Tories, only to vote his usual way when he got there (19,289). He has no patience with the shortcomings of his fellow men, expecting from them the same high standards that he sets himself.

Though witty in speech, as illustrated by his command of the crowd at election time, and by remarks such as those made on the drive to Candleford on the first morning the family goes there, he is totally unable to laugh at himself, being in fact prickly and over-defensive. This is shown in the quarrel with Uncle James Dowland (21,310). This serious approach is sometimes ridiculed by Flora Thompson; and there is often irony in the discrepancy between his abstract theories and his practice.

Clearly he is a kind man. One of Laura's earliest memories is of being taken by her father to collect pine cones (17,269), and she remembers that he often lifted her up to scratch the pig (p.271). He is strict with the children indoors in the way common to Victorian fathers, and we are told he is often 'cross' (2,34). But Laura is in the habit of regularly asking him if she may go to the Methodist services on Sunday evening (of which she knows he disapproves), so she is clearly not too much in awe of him or his pronouncements (14,215).

Gradually, though, as the trilogy progresses, it becomes clear that his inability to tolerate the limitations of people, and of life, is embittering his whole outlook. He has lost the ability to see the good in anyone – eventually all are knaves or fools in his view. And his political views can perhaps be seen as an expression of the whole man – a personal statement of an attitude to life, in the way that the mother's conservatism is basic to her nature.

The father is strongly linked with his daughter as the other true outsider to the hamlet, not only in intellect but in other aspects of his character. And Flora Thompson's love for her father is movingly conveyed in the scene where Laura, revisiting Lark Rise from Candleford Green, sees him obviously waiting in the lane to greet her, but pretending to be considering a broken branch. He cannot talk about his feelings openly, but his great pleasure in seeing her is almost painful to witness in so inhibited a man, particularly when he hurriedly tries to hide it by a quick return to his usual sardonic manner (38,510).

Laura

'Odd', the neighbours called her when discussing her in her presence (17,268).

In the portrait of Laura – the artist as a young girl – there are strong echoes of the Ugly Duckling theme. From an early age everything about her has marked her out as 'different'. She is not conventionally pretty by hamlet standards, being thin and leggy (she is several times compared to a heron, a moll heron or molern in dialect: see 5,95; 30,392). She likes reading and quiet contemplation, and is made unhappy by boisterous play requiring self-assertion. Above all she is set apart by her hypersensitive reactions to everyday life. This intensity of response is seen in a constant variety of experiences: her feelings about the countryside, its colours and its changing moods, and her pleasure in its beauties; her observation of the neighbours, their behaviour and their lifestyle; her feelings about her family; her reaction to the pig-killing and to the unthinking brutality of the bullying on the way to and from school.

Though neighbours often show a rough kindness to Laura, it is clear that, as a child, she makes people feel uneasy: she does not fit readily into the hamlet mothers' conception of childhood. Also, by being different, she perhaps represents an oblique criticism of their own more boisterous offspring, especially when she effortlessly masters such skills as reading. Her own mother would obviously feel happier if only Laura were able to fit more easily into what is looked upon as normal behaviour. Significantly, Laura as a child prefers the company of the older people in the hamlet, who are more able to accept her as she is; who praise her for her intelligence and discretion; and who seem to find her company congenial (Chapter 5).

But, as she grows older, we see the qualities that have, in early childhood, been of social disadvantage gradually becoming a source of strength, and of attraction to others. In Chapter 23 we are given a description of how school gradually becomes less of a nightmare as Laura gains the reputation of being a good listener, simply because she is quiet; and once she leaves the hamlet for wider horizons she finds herself appreciated in many ways. She is extremely popular with her Candleford cousins because, though clever, she is good-natured. She has many friends in the village, being habitually kind, tactful and helpful; and though her mother still despairs of her looks (30,393), Laura is obviously not unattractive – as shown by the Philip White episode in Chapter 38. *Lark Rise to Candleford* is not a fairytale, however, and though the duckling becomes to some extent a swan, it is against a very realistic background.

In presenting Laura, Flora Thompson is obviously aware of the danger of alienating the reader's sympathy by making the character too precious, too intense, too much the sensitive heroine. This she counteracts in several ways. Firstly, she uses humour. There is nobody in the book she laughs at more consistently than herself (Laura). (Her method of recording the far-from-flattering comments on her appearance made by her mother and the hamlet women is similar to that used by Chaucer in the Prologue to *The Canterbury Tales* where he seeks to disparage himself as a figure in the group.) There is often humour in the discrepancy between what the child might reasonably have expected to happen and what does in fact happen. For example, Laura's undoubted intelligence does not endear her to her elders: she receives no praise for learning to read at an early age; rather are her efforts frowned upon by other mothers (even the good-natured Mrs Braby) and go unrecognized by her teacher. Then there is humour in the contrast between her imaginative schemes and their prosaic enactment (a technique also used in presenting Edmund): for example, her attempts at tightrope walking on a gate (15,246); on her bright idea for making her appearance less odd by darkening her hair with ink (17,268).

The author's second method of making the character seem acceptably human is by stressing the normality of many aspects of her childhood, particularly her enjoyment of less strenuous pursuits: dancing, flower-collecting, skating. Though timid by nature, she has a mind of her own and a love of new experiences that can, on occasion, bring her into conflict with authority. For instance, curiosity leads her into going with Martha for the interview for a 'petty' place, though she has led her mother into believing she is going into the market town to do some shopping (Chapter 10). Similarly, in *Candleford Green* she cannot resist reading *Don Juan* at every opportunity, though she has been forbidden to do so, and is nearly caught at a double sin – she is particularly fond of reading the 'terrible book' in bed! (31,414–15.) Her childhood is also normal in that, however fine her sensibilities, she is forced to compromise early with the realities of country life: this is demonstrated at the end of Chapter 17; and there is a wealth of symbolic meaning in her enjoyment of the sweetbread.

Finally, the author secures our sympathy for Laura because she never defends her openly as a character – her virtues emerge from various episodes, but we are left to draw our own conclusions. This is well illustrated by the incident on the road to Candleford when the children walk there by themselves (25,338). She describes how Laura tries to sulk after Edmund calls her a coward, but is unable to keep up the mood for long – adding hastily that this is not from generosity of heart, for she seldom forgives an injury, but because she is always anxious to be liked. This readiness to be the first to criticize her own shortcomings adds to the general appeal of the character, particularly in view of the fact that Edmund's judgement is seen, in a wider context, to be only partially true. Laura may have been physically timid, but she was no moral coward: she remonstrates with the boys over the bird-nesting (9,152); and turns down Lady Adelaide's invitation to join the right-wing Primrose League, realizing that a matter of principle is involved (35,465–6). She is an outstandingly attractive character, primarily because her presentation is oblique.

Edmund

Edmund did not learn to read quite so early; but when he did, he learned more thoroughly (2,44).

The character of Edmund is based on Flora Thompson's younger brother Edwin Timms. (During the course of the book we learn that he fulfilled his wish to travel; he went to South Africa, India, Canada, and finally to his 'soldier's grave' in Belgium (2,47). The tablet commemorating his death in the First World War can be seen in the church at Cottisford (see the section on *Setting*). His mother received a pension from the Canadian Government, indicating that he emigrated but never married.)

In *Lark Rise to Candleford* Edmund is shown to have many positive qualities. While sharing the highly moral character of his sister – a source of considerable support during their childhood – his temperament is quite different. Thus, though not a cruel child, he is (unlike Laura) able to watch the pig-killing in the hamlet, seeing it as an exciting, imaginative event (1,26). Although he is younger than Laura, he never becomes her responsibility, being, from an early age, well able to look after himself. He is observant, and thoughtful in his approach to life (17,267–8). He is able to apply his intelligence to practical matters, and is later known locally as 'Solomon' (3,55). He is thorough in all he undertakes; for instance, when he decides, as a young man in the 1890s to emigrate with his younger brother (a character not developed in the book), he finds out all he can about farming, in practice as well as in theory (3,53).

Like Laura, as a child he appreciates his natural surroundings, but the difference between the two children is symbolically illustrated by their walk through the cornfield (15,234). Laura's reaction is aesthetic, Edmund's practical. He is enraged when she treads on the growing corn to collect wild flowers. Though he reacts with enjoyment to a line of poetry or a natural scene, he does not become over-involved: such things are an objective source of pleasure and satisfaction, as are more physical pursuits. But the fact that he is open about the range of his interests in an environment where the sexes were so rigidly role-conditioned is an early indication of his independence and integrity of mind. He appears in the trilogy as someone who always 'knows where he is going'. When attacked on the way to school, his automatic reaction is to fight back; years later he is able to run his life in his own way, devoid of his sister's feelings of guilt or inadequacy for their failure to satisfy their mother's ambitions for them.

Edmund always speaks his mind and lets others make what they will of it (25,338). This trait is occasionally used in the trilogy for humorous effect, particularly when it challenges the mother's strictly conventional approach, as in his reaction to her comment on the drunken hunchback (14,213). The essential humanity of this remark from a boy of ten, together with his strength of character, are qualities in Edmund that raise him to heroic stature.

Edmund is presented entirely for our admiration. Flora Thompson saw her brother as combining all virtue, a kind of masculine, tough-tender ideal, and her portrait of him in the book is a moving tribute to his memory. The characterization is without irony, but humour is often used to show that he is no sensitive soul shrinking from life but full of high spirits. That he is capable of temper is demonstrated when he chases Laura's friend round the garden – though he is supposed to be ill in bed with measles – furious that she has borrowed his Bible without permission (24,332). He is great fun as a companion, with his relish for the dramatic flourish (24,331; 333), and for escapades. Flora Thompson's other method of presentation is by contrast, either with herself or with the other boys: for example, Johnny, the Candleford cousin (22,314). As in this case, Edmund always comes off best in any comparison. Finally, the author shows how others were naturally drawn to Edmund. He is physically attractive (17,268), and personally popular; he is a favourite with his mother, and with the neighbours, and he fits in easily at school.

Other characters

Dorcas Lane

Ordinarily quietly observant, those eyes could disconcert with a flash of recognition of motives, sparkle with malice, or, more rarely, soften with sympathy (30,394).

Miss Lane is based partly on Mrs Whitton (an old friend of Flora Thompson's mother) who ran the post office/forge at Fringford, where she first worked (see the section on *The author and her work*), and partly on a postmistress in Surrey (*Purely for Pleasure*). She is one of the few characters in the book that we hear about before meeting. Laura and Edmund and their cousins are invited to visit her for the day during one of their summer holidays. Of the cousins, only Molly will go: the rest refuse, claiming that Miss Lane is 'faddy and old-fashioned' (27,361). Set against this is the fact that the end house children have heard from their parents that Miss Lane has a new telegraph machine and they find the prospect of seeing this exciting. This preview of Miss Lane is perhaps meant to be symbolic, for she combines in essence the spirit of the old and the new. This is reinforced later by the symbolism of her clocks: the grandfather clock in the domestic quarters is kept half an hour fast, in accordance with the old country custom, while the post office clock shows correct Greenwich time, received by wire at ten o'clock every morning (27,364).

Her modernity of outlook is shown initially by the fact that she has carried on the business in her own name after her father's death. A draper's shop or a grocer's might be inherited by a woman, but a blacksmith's was regarded as a sacrosanct traditional male stronghold. Her disregard for convention and independence of mind were shown in other ways: her dress was different, for she had a preference for bright silks that were thought daring (27,362); she was something of a bluestocking, and read *The Times* and Darwin in her free time. Most of all, she had a genuine interest in business and a fine head for it. Apart from running the post office/forge efficiently, she had shares in railways and the local canal company, and liked to keep an eye on the stock market. Intellectual in an abstract way, she was also shrewd in her dealings with people, instinctively grasping the workings of their minds.

Miss Lane is described in terms of nature imagery and vivid colour, which reinforces this impression of sharpness and alertness: 'a little, birdlike woman', in a 'kingfisher' silk dress, with 'snapping black eyes' (27,363). Her great love of the past and tradition is shown in the way she has kept the house and furniture as she had inherited it from her parents and grandparents, and in the way she organizes the domestic arrangements. Far from being the radical one might have been led to expect, she takes a very conservative, even authoritarian, line in such matters.

Though she likes to speak her mind plainly (see her reply to the unfortunate postman, Thomas Brown, 31,407), clearly her bark is worse than her bite, and a variety of incidents are included to illustrate her kindness. At the same time, there are many slyly satirical touches in her portrait. She is rather officious, having a decided view of her own importance as postmistress. She terrifies poor Laura on her first day as assistant by talk of busy periods and rush hours; and her ego must be handled with tact – Laura has to be careful not to become *too* popular with the customers or to take the initiative too openly (38,505–6).

Finally, though her essential generosity is acknowledged, some of her charitable gestures have mixed motives: a delicious tea greets Laura on her arrival at the post office, but, Miss Lane consumes the lion's share, without seeming to notice that Laura is too nervous to eat (30,397). Similarly, when anyone in the village is convalescing, she sends them a chicken dinner, but (as Flora Thompson comments slyly) always keeps the best cut from the breast for herself (32,429).

Structurally, Miss Lane plays an important role as a substitute mother figure for Laura in her teens. She is very fond of Laura, and helps her to develop socially and intellectually. She cares little about what others think of her actions (27,365), and acts as a liberating force for Laura, who has been taught by her mother to keep on good terms with everybody. She encourages Laura to read widely – and reverses her mother's creed by condemning fine needlework as a waste of time! (27,370.) She is presented in the trilogy as the classic authority figure, firm but just, providing a positive value that others can ridicule or react against, while they remain secure in the knowledge that the quality itself is indestructible.

Relatives

In presenting the relatives of the end house family, Flora Thompson widens the social context and gives a broader view of Victorian society. Neither of Flora Thompson's parents was born in the hamlet, and they had no family ties there. Her mother's parents lived reasonably near, for in Chapter 5 she describes how the child Laura spends many happy hours in their overgrown garden, and, before the grandfather becomes crippled by rheumatism, he visits the family daily. He has his own small business, buying and selling eggs locally, until the death of his horse brings an end to his ability to carry on the trade.

All the relatives are presented in terms of *contrast*, and this is particularly marked in the portraits of the *grandfather* and *grandmother*. The grandfather is a deeply religious man, and was a well-known local Methodist preacher in his younger days. He was also a practising Christian, in that he loves to give; and was prepared to accept the sacrifice of his violin, which he valued deeply, without complaint or self-pity. His slow death from crippling rheumatism is described in terms of martyrdom. The spiritual life-style he represents is set against the grandmother's material approach, for nobody could have been more involved with this world rather than the next. She was a pretty, vain woman, very much concerned with her own physical comfort and the keeping up of appearances. The contrast is symbolized in cultural terms – her husband plays the violin while she reads novelettes. But Flora Thompson's attitude is more subtle than one of straightforward moral censure or approval – Laura's reaction to the selling of the violin seems designed to represent a more balanced view of her grandfather's stance. The grandparents represent two extremes of behaviour, neither of which is totally condoned, for the grandmother is over-indulged by her husband's altruism, and it seems to be suggested that the end result is not very constructive for anybody.

The father's parents do not feature in the book, but his sisters are presented in varying degrees of detail. Of the three, Aunt Jane is mentioned most briefly, in Chapter 2, and Aunt Ann and her family are portrayed most fully, for their house became a second home for Laura for several years during the summer holidays.

The two Candleford households of *Aunt Ann* and *Aunt Edith*, and their occupants, are brilliantly juxtaposed in Chapters 21 and 22 of *Over to Candleford.* In a sense, their presentation is another variation of the 'old versus new' theme, recurrent in the trilogy, for though both sets of relatives were welcoming to the hamlet family, well-meaning and generous, at the Dowlands they see displayed all the worst traits of the 'nouveau riche', the whole aim being to impress the visitors; at the home of Uncle Tom, the country shoemaker, everything is done to make the family feel at ease. The author sets the formal against the informal, social behaviour against spontaneity: in terms of the houses themselves; the appearance of the occupants; the meals offered; the manner in which visitors are entertained; the indoor setting of one, as opposed to the other's easy access to the garden. The presentation of the Dowland family is clearly satirical by comparison with that of the second family of relatives. *Uncle Tom and Aunt Ann represent a criterion of moral value* in the trilogy, and are the epitome of true kindness and generosity. It has been suggested by H. J. Massingham that Uncle Tom has more specific symbolic weight – that he is the best of the old way of life of Old England, the last of a long line (Introduction, p.11). Certainly Tom's pride in his work, his integrity, his liberal approach to life are all carefully established in the trilogy.

In acting as substitute parents for Laura, Aunt Ann and Uncle Tom have a liberating effect emotionally. Both Laura's parents are very inhibited about feelings and strict over discipline. Aunt Ann is very demonstrative in her affection, and both she and her husband have a relaxed attitude to their children, encouraging them to express their views and develop as individuals (see Chapters 22 and 25). The precision of Flora Thompson's method of character portrayal can be seen in the contrasted *physical* appearance of the two families of relatives. Note particularly how she draws on the conventional idea of the fat jolly aunty in describing Aunt Edith, but reveals merely by juxtaposition how her appearance, 'pink and plump' with a 'grey' dress and 'grey' hair (21,308) is really an indication of the flabbiness of her mental outlook, compared with the clear-cut lines of Aunt Ann's appearance and moral character (22,313).

Neighbours

The group that predominates as an entity under this heading comprises *the people of Lark Rise*. The fullest descriptions are given in Chapters 3, 4, 14, and 16. In *Lark Rise to Candleford* the hamlet people are depicted as the 'salt of the earth': hardworking, stoical, outspoken, fond of gossip, drink and entertainment; but unpretentious and seemingly unperturbed by any system, natural or man-made. In any class conflict, they invariably come off best – they are shown as defeating authority by openly questioning it, ignoring it, or ridiculing it among themselves. As one would expect, the behaviour of the children at school reflects the way they are brought up at home (11,182, 186), and in their attempts to muster a congregation, both Miss Ellison and Mr Marley come up against attitudes that are far from obsequious (1,32; 14,226). The hamlet-dwellers who go to church are unmoved by the Rev Ellison's rhetoric as he lectures them on the divine rightness of the class system as it exists because they simply take no notice of him: they either nod off as he begins the familiar theme, or they are too busy eyeing their neighbours' Sunday-best clothes (14,211–13). The farmer had to be treated with a certain amount of respect as their employer, but his bailiff was mocked as soon as his back was turned (3,55).

Though the hamlet people act as a definite force in the trilogy, they are not idealized as a group. The author describes them in Chapter 14 as 'fallible human beings' (p.220) and emphasizes that, though they carry out St Paul's injunction to weep with those who weep, showing an endless sympathy when their neighbours are in trouble, they find it harder to rejoice with those who rejoice. In fact, there is nothing they dislike more than seeing someone from their own class doing better than themselves. This is shown in many incidents, e.g. the jealousy over the Scripture prize (12,192), and the cool reception given the girl who makes a socially advantageous marriage (10,166). With its faults and its virtues, their lifestyle acts as a basic criterion by which Laura judges all subsequent social behaviour. The people's lack of affectation, their being exactly what they seemed, provides her with an anchor in later life.

Flora Thompson gives particular attention to the two older

women of Lark Rise, *Old Sally and Queenie*, who, H. J. Massingham suggests, share with Laura's Uncle Tom the symbolic representation of 'Old England'. Both are described in detail in Chapter 5, and there are other scattered references. *Old Sally* is the village matriarch. Apart from the inn, her house is the largest in Lark Rise and, more importantly, she owns it and the land it is built on; and she has a small private income, inherited from her father. With this and the produce from their garden, she and her husband Dick are able to manage more comfortably than many others in the hamlet and, unlike most of the older inhabitants, have no fear of the workhouse.

Old Sally has an important function in the book: it is through her that the reader learns the past history of Lark Rise; she can remember a time before the heath was enclosed (see the section on *Historical Setting*). Socially Sally and her husband are no longer typical of the hamlet folk. The author stresses that they have more of everything than anybody else, including roses in profusion and beautiful old furniture. Recorded snatches of conversation indicate clearly that such abundance does not altogether make the old couple popular; nor does the fact that they are secretive about their affairs and hold themselves aloof from their neighbours. Apart from her symbolic role in the trilogy, Old Sally is definitely recollected as a striking individual. She is by nature strong-willed and domineering, shown in her relationship with her husband. As well as metaphorically, 'wearing the trousers', she also literally sports a moustache (p.76). Whatever sterling qualities her upbringing may have bred in Sally, sympathy for her less well-placed fellow men does not seem to be among them. She has nothing but contempt for the younger hamlet women who have large families they can ill afford to keep, having prudently restricted her own to two.

In depicting Old Sally, Flora Thompson comes up against the problem of sympathetically portraying an admirable character who is yet rather daunting. In contrast, *Queenie* is much more engaging on a human level. Initially, she gains sympathy because she is as concerned as anybody in the hamlet with trying to make ends meet, and in this she is hindered rather than helped by her husband, *Twister* (the fact that he wanders the hamlet in a state of advanced psychosis throws an interesting light on the discrepancy between the general and the particular, the tale and the teller; since in Chapter 1 we have been assured that, 'nervous troubles, there as elsewhere, had yet to be invented', p.19). Queenie's virtues and skills are many – she is always warm and welcoming to the end house children, and ready patiently to explain her bee-keeping methods and demonstrate her lace-making. Incidental touches in the portrait bring her endearingly to life: for example, her concern for her pig (1,31), and her fondness for snuff (5,88). Like Old Sally, she has additional importance as a character in that she fills in the history of the hamlet, as she can remember former, more prosperous, times.

As neighbours, Old Sally and Queenie are juxtaposed firmly against the sort of neighbour Laura is increasingly to meet as she moves away from the social scene of her youth to a life in suburbia – typified by *Mrs Green* of Candleford Green villas (39,531–5). Mrs Green, too, is houseproud; she likes to keep herself to herself and, like Old Sally, believes in limiting her family. But Flora Thompson expends considerable skill in making clear that in her view everything about Mrs Green is false and artificial. She subjects Mrs Green's house, its furnishings, her attitudes and her appearance to quite merciless satire (for example, though the house is spotless, she notes that her teeth are decaying). This is all the more marked in view of the author's earlier generosity when recording the Lark Rise inhabitants; in portraying in Mrs Green everything she dislikes about suburban life, she comes close to presenting a caricature rather than a character.

Between the two extremes represented by Old Sally and Queenie on the one hand, and Mrs Green on the other, there are many individual neighbours and friends recollected with affection and occasionally satire. Particularly memorable are *Bertha*, the maid from Candleford, *Willy*, the friend from Candleford Green, *Matthew*, *Zillah* and *Mrs Macey* (see the opening remarks in this section on *Characters*).

Authority figures

These are the 'bettermost people' encountered in church, school and in the local society.

In *religion*, *Mr Ellison* is a parson of the old school (11,179). He has little in common with his parishioners, and his main concern is to impress on them from the pulpit and in Scripture lessons the necessity for keeping to the established social system; he seems to have no interest in their spiritual welfare. Apart from his autocratic ideas, he is a kindly and charitable man: in personal contact with his parishioners in their homes, he is as embarrassed as they by the dearth of topics for small talk; and the conclusion of each visit brings feelings of mutual relief. His portrait is satirical but affectionate, as is that of his daughter *Miss Ellison*. She is well-intentioned but tactless – consequently much of her kindness goes unappreciated by the hamlet women. Fortunately, like her father, she is not a reflective person, and is never hurt by the evasive tactics brought into play when she visits Lark Rise, she never realizes she is not welcome. When Laura first moves to Candleford Green, the vicar there is, *Mr Coulsdon*, who has similar social attitudes to those she has observed in the Rector. He is however, a less formidable character because he possesses neither the Old Testament fire and fury of Mr Ellison in the pulpit, nor his dominating physical presence. Nevertheless, he too urged his parishioners to adhere to the social system as it stood; and he provided charity for the poor and the sick on a generous scale. His wife, *Mrs Coulsdon*, who is the grand-daughter of an earl, supports his view on social superiority, but is not averse to joining the villagers in gossip when it suits her purpose. She is portrayed as a less attractive character than her husband (32,424–6). After their death, *Mr and Mrs Delafield* take over the living, and their coming marks a transition from the old ways (Chapter 39). They scandalized the traditional element in the village by their informal approach to life and to their role in the community, and they provide a rich source of humour. They make no secret of their poverty and meet their parishioners as equals. The Sunday sermons become devoted to matters of everyday morality.

In *education* a similar mellowing process can be seen. The three schoolmistresses described in Chapter 11 (see summary) underline the theme of social change. There is a nice irony in the portrait of the third schoolmistress, Miss Shepherd, who, though as an authority figure she provides a compromise between the conservative ways of Miss Holmes and the radical approach of Miss Higgs, is, in her personal character, a Socialist with snobbish tendencies; for this she is gently mocked (12,196–7).

The remaining group are basically *social superiors*, which includes the gentry. Brief mention must be made of the farmer at Fordlow, important in the hamlet as the employer of the men. He is more openly criticized by Flora Thompson than is anyone else in this group: she records in a bitterly ironic tone his view of himself as the liberal dispenser of weekly wages and the harvest-home supper (3,61). *Mr Morris* the farm bailiff (nicknamed by the men 'Old Monday Morning'), is presented in a more kindly light, being shown as subject to exploitation in much the same way as are the men.

Squire Bracewell is a popular local figure, being brash, friendly and unpretentious – unlike his mother *Mrs Bracewell*, whose 'Lady of the Manor' approach includes little tact, even less genuine concern, and much criticism. Both are fully described in Chapter 12; and in their portraits Flora Thompson seems to be underlining the fact that both lack the moral refinement that she later finds in the aristocracy she meets in Candleford Green. The Squire is jolly, but he is also shown to be rather vulgar; and Mrs Bracewell's airs and graces conceal a narrow-minded outlook. In contrast, *Sir Timothy* and *Lady Adelaide* of Candleford Green are presented as essentially courteous people, and charming in the best sense of the word. Both are drawn without satire and with the evident approval of the author, and in themselves represent the best of aristocratic values.

Chapter summaries, textual notes and revision questions

Lark Rise

1, Poor People's Houses

In the 1880s, the period during which this part of the trilogy is set, the hamlet of Lark Rise, in the north-east of Oxfordshire, consists of about thirty cottages and an inn, built more or less in a circle and surrounded by a deeply rutted cart-track known as 'the Rise'. Most of the men are employed as farm labourers at a weekly wage of ten shillings. One house, known as the 'end house', is set slightly apart from the others and, when the book begins, is the home of the stonemason, his wife and their two small children: Laura aged three, and Edmund a year and a half younger. The stone cottages, comprising one or two bedrooms with one room downstairs, frequently house families with eight or more children. Sanitary conditions are primitive: none of the cottages has indoor lavatories or running water; indeed, only three have their own well.

It is suggested by the author that the possible unhealthy effects of overcrowding in such conditions at the time of the trilogy were offset by the open-air life led by most of the inhabitants and by the fact that cleanliness was highly regarded. Many of the cottages were rented for one or two shillings a week. The rest of the chapter is taken up with a detailed account of the domestic and economic arrangements necessary for families to survive on the eight or nine shillings that remained. The importance of the pig's well-being is stressed, bacon providing the basic meat; and a pig-killing is vividly described.

Flora Thompson is at pains to emphasize the quality of the life she is portraying. The hamlet dwellers were, she claims, poor but happy.

Lark Rise Flora Thompson's name for Juniper Hill (see the map and section on *Setting*). Margaret Lane notes that Lark Rise was actually the name of the field by the cottage where the Timms family lived (*Purely for Pleasure*).

arable Ploughed or ploughable land, here devoted to 'corn and root crops, chiefly wheat' (3,50).

'Hundred Acres' All the fields had names, which often referred to their history, but sometimes to their size, as here (3,52).

juniper bushes Evergreen shrubs with prickly leaves and dark purplish berries.

furzy Gorse covered.

common land ... so ceded See *Setting*.

mother village 'Fordlow' in the book, Flora Thompson's name for Cottisford (see map and *Setting*).

the turnpike Formerly a road with gates for the collection of tolls, but used here to mean main road or highway.

market town Brackley (see map and *Setting*).

gig Light two-wheeled carriage drawn by one horse.

shakedowns Straw or blankets spread on the floor as beds.

Gentle Jesus Child's prayer written by Charles Wesley (1707–88), brother of John Wesley, founder of the Methodists. It was published in *Hymns and Sacred Poems* (1742):

> Gentle Jesus, meek and mild,
> Look upon a little child;
> Pity my simplicity,
> Suffer me to come to Thee.

'ooman's work i.e. woman's work.

raddled Coloured with raddle, i.e. red ochre.

The Bombardment of Alexandria ... boiling sea Contemporary catastrophes. In 1882 in Alexandria, an important Egyptian port, there were anti-foreign riots and the town was subsequently bombarded by the British. On 28 December 1879 the Tay bridge, which crosses the Firth of Tay at Dundee, collapsed during a storm causing the loss of ninety lives.

Mr Gladstone William Ewart Gladstone (1809–98) entered Parliament as a Tory in 1833, but became the leading personality of the Liberal Party from 1868 until his retirement in 1894. He was a noted reformer and served as Prime Minister four times.

Lord Salisbury Robert Arthur Talbot Gascoyne-Cecil, 3rd Marquess of Salisbury (1830–1903) was a Conservative politician who entered Parliament in 1853. He was Prime Minister on three occasions and his governments were responsible for such reforms as the reorganization of local government (1888), free public education (1891) and workmen's compensation (1897).

Lord Randolph Churchill Lord Randolph Henry Spencer Churchill (1849–95) was a prominent Tory politician who was Chancellor of the Exchequer and leader of the House of Commons (1886). Because of its proposed cuts in funds for the armed services, his first budget was unpopular with the cabinet; and he resigned, spending the remainder of his political career on the back benches. He was the father of Sir Winston Churchill.

the muck'll i.e. the muck-hill.

sow thistle Common weed with thistle-like leaves containing a milky juice.

victuals Food, provisions.

chitterlings A name commonly applied to the small intestines (usually of pigs) when they have been cooked for food.

traveller's joy Wild climbing plant (*Clematis vitalba*) which towards the end of the summer is characterized by trailing wisps resembling sheep's wool.

flitches Side of salted and cured pork.

hobnailed dreadnoughts Heavy boots, the soles of which were protected by nails with massive heads.

catechumens Pupils undergoing instruction prior to confirmation.

2, A Hamlet Childhood

A favourite walk taken by the children at the end house is: out of the hamlet, then along the main road, past the milestone which tells them that Oxford (where their father lived as a child) is 19 miles away. They go as far as a grassy clearing where they pick mushrooms and flowers and occasionally see a gipsy encampment. Their mother pushes the pram containing Edmund or, later, the baby May. Once they are accompanied by their father's sister Aunt Jane, who is married to a master-builder in Yorkshire. On the walk, Laura senses that her mother dislikes her sister-in-law, and this is confirmed later when her mother scoffs at the aunt's talk of her clever relations. We are told something of the mother's own educational background, unusual for a girl of her class, and of the fact that she was later a children's nurse in a local Rectory. She brings professional standards to the upbringing of her own children. The other hamlet children are less gently reared, the general practice being to send pre-school children out 'to play' unsupervised, whatever the weather, for the whole day. Laura and Edmund says it'll ruin her eyes.

are sometimes allowed to join them, though their father was reluctant for them to mix locally. He has always intended to move from Lark Rise before the children start school, but the years pass. In order to gain more time, he proposes educating the children at home – in practice this means that Laura teaches herself to read. This causes some talk in the hamlet, and eventually a neighbour reports the family to the Attendance Officer. So Laura, and later Edmund and the others, have to go to the local school in the village of Fordlow.

bassinet Type of child's pram resembling a wicker cradle on wheels.
toque A small hat, often without a brim.
Miss Braddon Mary Elizabeth Braddon (1837–1915), author of more than eighty novels and particularly famous for the melodramatic *Lady Audley's Secret* (1862).
We are Seven Title of a poem published in 1798 by William Wordsworth (1770–1850).
glees Songs for three or more voices, usually sung without instrumental accompaniment.
Michaelmas Day 29 September (a quarter-day).
dirty heads i.e. head lice ('nits').
School Attendance Office See *Setting*.
Mavor's First Reader A child's primer.
Pilgrim's Progress Famous religious allegory by John Bunyan (1628–88).
Grimm's *Fairy Tales* Folk tales collected by the German brothers Grimm, first published in 1812.
Gulliver's Travels An account of four imaginary voyages written by Jonathan Swift (1667–1745), first published in 1726. It has always been a popular book with children, though it was intended as satire.
The Daisy Chain Sentimental novel about a large motherless family, published in 1856 by Charlotte M. Yonge (1823–1901).
Mrs Molesworth's ...*Carrots* Mary Louisa Molesworth (1839–1921) was a prolific writer of children's books, including *Carrots; Just a Little Boy* (1876) and *The Cuckoo Clock* (1877), concerning a child's adventures in a fantasy world entered through an old cuckoo clock.
spoor Track.
dust thou art ... return Genesis, 3,19.
okkard i.e. awkward.

3, Men Afield

The village of Fordlow, a mile and a half from Lark Rise in the opposite direction to the Oxford road, is described as smaller than the hamlet but contains the church and the Rectory, the school, and the farmhouse that is the working headquarters for most of the men and boys from the hamlet. The appearance, dress, speech and general philosophy of the farm labourer of that time is described. Stoical endurance of the hard life is the most highly prized virtue. The farming day is outlined, the dinner hour with its 'men's tales' forming the highlight. Several middle-aged women, bored at home, do part-time field work. They are: Mrs Spicer, symbolically distinguished by her wearing of trousers; Lily, a rough, illiterate, unmarried mother; and the sentimental Mrs Braby, avid reader of novelettes. One man, 'Algy', works with the women. He is something of a social outcast, apparently an upper-class army deserter. The men are paid on Friday evening by the farmer, who is, on the whole, liked by his men, being associated in their minds rather with the pleasures than the pains of their employment. They direct their resentment against his bailiff Mr Morris, nicknamed 'Old Monday'. The custom is for the men to give their wives the weekly wage and receive back a shilling pocket-money. The men's working day is finished off with an hour or two spent on their own gardens or allotments. This chapter ends, like Chapter 1, with the reflection that though the life is poor and hard, it is not unhappy.

mullioned windows Windows divided by vertical stone bars.

stuck up Conceited, snobbish.

Remember Job Old Testament patriarch who displayed great patience in adversity (see the book of Job).

Mr Frederick Grisewood Frederick Henry Grisewood (1888–1972) was a well-known member of the Outside Broadcasts Department of the BBC from 1929 to 1948.

Hodge Traditional name for a farm labourer or country yokel, occuring in English literature from the sixteenth century onwards (e.g. in the play *Gammer Gurton's Needle*, first performed 1566) and common in the nineteenth century (e.g. Richard Jefferies' *Hodge and his Masters*, 1880).

Thomas Hardy's Wessex The novelist and poet Thomas Hardy (1840–1928) was born in Dorset, the region he later called Wessex in his novels about pastoral life.

sainfoin Pink-flowered herb grown for fodder.

The Osiers A field containing willows.

hemmed i.e. damned.

twitch Twitch grass or couch grass, a weed with long creeping roots.

yarns i.e. earns.

cut chaff i.e. chopped hay and straw for use as cattle food.

Solomon King of Israel (c.970–933 BC), son of David and famed for his wisdom (see Kings 1).

old turnip-faced watches Slang term for large thick old-fashioned watches.

Decameron Boccaccio's *Decameron*, written in the mid fourteenth century, is a collection of tales, many of which are famous for their bawdy qualities.

mangel A large kind of beet used as cattle food.

Bow Bells* and the *Family Herald Penny weeklies which began in the mid nineteenth century and featured romantic stories about the aristocracy. *Bow Bells* was later incorporated in *Duchess Novelettes* (the grandmother was also fond of these weeklies; see 5,94).

dogcart Two-wheeled horse-drawn cart (originally with a compartment for dogs).

4, At the 'Wagon and Horses'

The taproom of the 'Wagon and Horses' forms a social club of sorts for the men of the hamlet. Here they congregate each evening to drink their half-pint, to discuss politics, to indulge in national and local gossip, and to sing. The songs are a mixture of the old and new, depending on the age of the contributor. Several examples of the most popular and recurrent ballads are recorded in full. Often the men have an unseen audience, as the inn-keeper's children listen on the stairs, and women and children gather outside on fine evenings to enjoy the free entertainment. At the conclusion of the chapter Flora Thompson voices regret at the passing of an age that knew, she feels, 'the now lost secret of being happy on little'.

close wi' their ha'pence i.e. stingy, mean.

Nigger Head brand A strong black plug tobacco.
Politics ... responsibility seriously See *Setting*.
Three Acres ... Disestablishment of the Church Contemporary political issues that divided public opinion in the 1880s. Charles Stewart Parnell (1846–91) was a member of a leading Anglo-Irish Protestant family and became the head of the controversial Home Rule for Ireland movement in 1877. In 1881 he was imprisoned for inciting the Irish to unrest, but was later released as the troubles grew. He remained a prominent political figure until 1890, when he was named by Captain O'Shea in his successful divorce suit against his wife Kitty.
Joseph Arch (1826–1919), farm labourer, lay preacher and founder of a union for agricultural workers in 1872.
gibbet Gallows.
Jack the Ripper Notorious undiscovered murderer of women in the East End of London between 1888 and 1891. His victims – all prostitutes – were appallingly mutilated.
Over the Garden Wall ... Eyes These music hall songs are an interesting illustration of the accuracy of Flora Thompson's dating, e.g. 'Two Lovely Black Eyes', itself a parody of 'My Nelly's Blue Eyes', was first sung by Charles Coborn on 21 May 1886 at the Paragon Music Hall, Mile End.
noggins A noggin is a small measure, usually a quarter of a pint.

5, Survivals

This chapter is devoted to a description of the old people of the hamlet whom the child Laura knows well. At that time, when the Lark Rise inhabitants grew too old to work, they had to rely on their children's charity or go to the workhouse, a dreaded fate. There are one or two lucky exceptions: Old Sally and her husband Dick were fortunate in that not only did they own their own house, but they had inherited seventy-five pounds. This capital they had managed to increase by careful saving during their working lives and by keeping their family to two children. Since both have limited literacy they enlist Laura's help in the management of their financial affairs. The accounts given to the child of the earlier, happier and more prosperous days of the hamlet – when the people had common grazing rights and greater economic independence and self-reliance – made a deep and lasting impression on her. Their house and garden is lovingly described.

Old Sally looked after geese before enclosure days.

Another favourite is Queenie, living behind the end house, and their closest neighbour. She keeps to the old country skills of bee-keeping and lace-making, and enthralls the children with tales of her younger days. But her husband Twister frightens them with his bizarre and finally psychotic behaviour. Another sad note is introduced with the tale of the Major, a kindly old soldier who lived alone and valued his independence, but who nevertheless died in the workhouse infirmary where he had been taken against his will. The chapter ends with a description of the grandparents, making clear Laura's preference for her grandfather. The author reflects on the difference that the introduction of the state Old Age pension made to the lives of the poor.

the workhouse Institutions provided in each district for the relief of the poor. They were organized on harsh lines and were often more feared than poverty itself.
dame school School for very small children (often run by an elderly woman) prior to the introduction of compulsory education as a public service.
hearthstone Stone for whitening hearths, floors etc.
sheep's-head clock A clock having the works exposed to view.
skep i.e. skip (a straw basket).
red pan roofs i.e. made of red earthenware.
linsey-woolsey Dress material of coarse wool woven on a cotton warp.
Hungry 'Forties Decade of 1840–9, a time of great distress for the British poor, principally because of poor harvests.
Bassalonies A reference to Barcelona nuts – hazelnuts imported from Spain.
gratis Free.
people were telling Queenie . . . put away i.e. they were saying he should be in a lunatic asylum.
snuff Tobacco in fine powder form.
the Prince Consort Prince Albert of Saxe-Coburg-Gotha (1819–61), husband of Queen Victoria.
a moll heron Dialect for a heron, a variant being 'a molern' (30,392).
melted into air, into thin air Reference to Shakespeare's *The Tempest*, IV,1,150.
Lord George David Lloyd George (1863–1945) famous Liberal politician, became Chancellor of the Exchequer in 1908, and advocated a series of social reforms, including the Old Age Pension Act, 1908.

6, The Besieged Generation

The chapter title refers to Laura's parents' generation. They are 'besieged' by poverty and were 'rich only in children'. The chapter describes how the women coped with life; it is the domestic equivalent of Chapter 3, 'Men Afield'. Tastes have changed since Old Sally set up home; and most young women prefer to furnish their houses with the mass-produced goods flooding the market, rejecting the hand-made products of an earlier age. But traditional values still hold: cleanliness is still regarded as a primary virtue; houses are vigorously cleaned daily; and Monday keeps its place as washing day. In the morning the arrival of a letter, or a parcel of clothes from a daughter in service, may make a welcome distraction. The morning's work done, a relatively pleasant period of light work, sewing or reading, follows. The afternoons are subject to irritating interruptions either from the gossips – the mournful Mrs Mullins or the scandal-mongering Mrs Andrews – or from the habitual borrowers. Most of the young women have been in service and reflect their employers' habits in their impromptu afternoon tea-parties, where fashion or the latest novelettes are discussed. Most of the women grow flowers and herbs which they use in making their own wines and jams; with which simple fare they make the occasional visitor welcome.

ridded up Dialect term for 'tidied up' or 'cleared up'.
thin-road i.e. flat as a fish that has hardly any roe.
bustles Pads of material worn under the skirt on the small of the back.
firmament Vault of heaven. Used here metaphorically.
chenille Yarn with pile protruding all round it.
Prince of Wales . . . old Queen Edward, Prince of Wales, born 1841, later reigned as Edward VII from 1901 to 1910. He was known to be a womanizer. 'The old Queen' was Queen Victoria (1819–1901).
mossel o' bread i.e. morsel of bread.
Richard's *Pamela* *Pamela, or Virtue Rewarded* (1740) by Samuel Richardson (1689–1761) is generally considered to be the first modern English novel. It was written in epistolary form and records how a young girl successfully warded off her employer's attempts at seduction. Her 'reward' was marriage.
Belzoni's *Travels* Giovanni Battista Belzoni (1778–1823), born in

Padua, came to England in 1803. In 1815 he went to Egypt where he devoted himself to the excavation of tombs, pyramids and temples, experiences described in his *Travels*, published in 1820.

The *Weekly Despatch* ... *News* Popular newspapers of the day. *Reynold's News* continued until 1962, when it changed its name to the *Sunday Citizen* and survived until 1967.

Hamlet's words ... handsaw Reference to Shakespeare's *Hamlet*, II,2,374–5.

a bit left-handed i.e. rather awkward, clumsy or improbable.

brassed up i.e. handed over their wages.

the women had ... not very effective The suggestion here is that the herb was used as part of their ineffectual attempts at contraception.

Yarrow (*Achillea millefolium.*) Sometimes known as 'milfoil'. A plant with small, usually white, flowers and finely divided leaves; frequently found at roadsides.

7, Callers

Any interruption from the outside world helps to break the monotony of the hamlet day, a point made in the previous chapter by reference to the eager anticipation of the daily post. Other regular callers are Jerry Parish, the fish and fruit man, arriving on Monday mornings to tempt the housewives with bloaters and oranges; and Mr Wilkins, the baker, who makes a delivery three times a week. The list of casual callers is much longer. Tinkers come, offering to mend pots and kettles, or to grind scissors and razors; gypsy women knock, selling cabbage-nets and pegs, and exchanging charming compliments for vegetables and old clothes. Their smooth-tongued wheedling is very different from the plain begging to which tramps and the homeless poor are reduced. Any kind of hire-purchase agreement is fated to be disastrous as far as the hamlet people are concerned, living as they do on such low fixed incomes, but this does not deter the more enthusiastic salesmen. Very occasionally the pedlar calls, bringing lengths of dress material, pins, cottons, and tapes. In summer the German band plays outside the inn, providing once-yearly free entertainment. For the marionette show, however, a penny admission is charged. The only other entertainment is the dancing bear, which the children from the end house encounter once on the road. They are lucky, too, that the one year the cheap-jack calls selling crockery, theirs is one of the only two families in the hamlet who are able to afford one of his 'luxury' items.

bloaters Salted and smoked herrings.
a John Dory An odd-looking fish with a very miserable expression. Grey or brown but with a conspicuous black spot behind the pectoral fins. Some versions have it that St Peter picked up the fish and left the marks.
hunch Thick piece.
Egyptian Egypt was the supposed origin of the gypsies when they first appeared in England in the early sixteenth century.
florin Coin worth two shillings or ten new pence.
threepenny bit Small coin, worth slightly more than one new penny.
tallyman Man who sells goods on credit.
girt i.e. great.

8, 'The Box'

Here matters related to health education are discussed: confinements for which the Rector's daughter lends 'the Box' of the title containing baby clothes; the role played by Mrs Quinton, the old lady who acts as midwife; breast-feeding, and post-natal care for the mother. The author then passed on to a more general consideration of the health of the hamlet-dwellers as a group, including such topics as personal hygiene; birth control (or the lack of it); and illegitimacy and the contradictory attitudes it then provoked, as did any extra-marital relationships. She concludes with the story of one unmarried mother who comes to live in the hamlet with her children. She is initially greeted with a hostility that changes to friendship when it becomes known that her son is a talented melodeon player, willing to provide music for the communal dancing in the summer evenings.

swathes Swaddling clothes, long pieces of material used to wrap round babies to restrain their movements.
barrows Sleeveless garments for babies.
knew their luck again i.e. knew they were pregnant again.
shortening i.e. when the child went into short clothes.

trigged out i.e. dressed or decked out.
lawn Fine woven linen or cotton.
Valenciennes A type of lace manufactured at Valenciennes, a town in Northern France.
half a crown Coin worth twelve and a half new pence.
Sairey Gamps Sarah Gamp, usually called Sairey as here, was the disreputable nurse in Dickens's *Martin Chuzzlewit*. Her name has become synonymous with slovenly midwifery.
Beecham's and Holloway's Pills . . . th'innards too Most of these medicines were designed to fulfil the same function as the old man's soapsuds.
rough music Sometimes known as a 'skimmity ride', as in Thomas Hardy's *The Mayor of Casterbridge*.
melodeon A kind of accordion.

9, Country Playtime

As well as enjoying dancing, the girls of the hamlet play the rhyming and singing games that have been handed down to them by tradition. Many are recorded, with the accompanying actions described. Marbles, skipping, hopscotch and dibs (or jacks) are also popular pastimes, together with making 'pin-a-sights' – little petal arrangements under glass. After they reach school age, the boys and girls no longer play together and the boys' games often become more aggressive. They are fond of bird-nesting and also bird trapping, though the latter 'sport' is not in fact confined to the boys alone, small birds being generally regarded as a tasty delicacy. Other spoils are more illicit: pheasants make an occasional appearance on the dinner table; and once Laura and Edmund witness the poaching of a hare.

In ten years' time . . . forgotten In two books, *The Lore and Language of Schoolchildren* (1959) and *Children's Games in Street and Playground* (1969), Iona and Peter Opie offer evidence that some of these games have, in various parts of the country, survived to the present day.
'nothing common did or mean' Line 57 of *An Horatian Ode upon Cromwell's Return from Ireland* written in 1650 by Andrew Marvell (1621–78). The line refers to Charles I.
Queen Anne, Queen Anne . . . Stuart monarchs Reference is made here to Anne of Denmark (1574–1619) who married James VI of Scotland (1566–1625) in 1589, before he became King James I of

England in 1603. The 'last of our Stuart monarchs' was Queen Anne (1665–1714), daughter of James II and Anne Hyde. This Queen Anne succeeded William III in 1702.

Queen Caroline Caroline of Brunswick (1768–1821) married George IV (then Prince of Wales) in 1795. The details of their unhappy marriage made a topic for common gossip for a long time.

Dibs Also known as 'five-stones' or 'jacks'.

Boy Scout movement Founded in 1908 by Robert Baden-Powell.

quod Slang for prison.

gargoyles A gargoyle is a spout, often with a grotesque human or animal head or mouth, projecting from the gutter of a building, to carry water away.

10, Daughters of the Hamlet

Whereas boys, when they left school at ten or eleven, could find immediate employment as farm labourers at a few shillings a week, the girls continued to be a 'burden' on their parents while they remained at home. It was the practice for them to look after the younger children of the family for perhaps a year, after which they would be put into service with a local tradesman or schoolmaster at what was known as a 'petty' place. Payment was low, a shilling a week being normal, plus some free clothes, but they would be gaining experience regarded as valuable. Laura once accompanies a friend, Martha, and her small brother Tommy, to an interview for such a place. After the year was up a permanent situation would be found for them, often some distance away. The girls began service as scullery-maids or as third or fourth housemaid in a big town or country house. They were usually very generous with their families, sending them money and clothes. The only time they would return to the hamlet was for the fortnightly summer holiday or for their wedding. Some girls married and settled away from the hamlet, but those who had formed early attachments waited eagerly for a house to fall vacant so that they could go back. (Chokey and Bess are the exception: their courtship lasts for eighteen years before their 'funny little wedding'.) Once back, the girls reverted to hamlet ways, but they had brought with them new ideas that influenced their lifestyle, and their relationship with their husbands became more of a partnership than in their parents' time.

petty places cf. French *petit*; meaning 'little'. Often applied in English to denote a lesser importance, e.g. petty officer.

garibaldi The small scarlet jacket was named after Guiseppe Garibaldi (1807–1882), Italian soldier and patriot who, with a thousand red-shirted followers, conquered Sicily and Naples in 1860, making Victor Emmanuel King of Italy.

Morning Post The *Morning Post*, a London daily newspaper founded in 1772 and amalgamated in 1937 with the *Daily Telegraph*.

the *Church Times* Founded in February, 1863, and still in publication.

serge Hard-wearing worsted cloth.

hip-bath A portable shallow bath.

When the Princess . . . Queen Alexandra Princess Alexandra (1844–1925) was the wife of Edward, Prince of Wales, later Edward VII, and daughter of Christian IX of Denmark. She was a noted beauty and leader of fashion.

cashmere Fine soft wool from the Kashmir goat, or an imitation.

a bit soft in the upper storey i.e. rather simple-minded.

Paisley Shawl made in a soft woollen material from the town of Paisley, Strathclyde, Scotland. The well-known 'Paisley pattern' of these shawls (and other garments such as men's silk ties and scarves) is said to be an adaptation of an original design from India.

windsor chairs Wooden chairs with a craved frame and upright rods as back support.

American cloth Cotton cloth onto which a waterproof shiny surface has been bonded.

antimacassars Protective coverings hung over the backs of chairs, originally to prevent their being stained by the Macassar oil used as a hair dressing by men.

cretonne Patterned cotton cloth.

keep out o' th' road i.e. keep out of the way.

11, School

The Lark Rise children walk a mile and a half every day to the local school at Fordlow. The walk is something of an ordeal for the more sensitive ones like Laura, and she dreads to think how Edmund will suffer in his turn. But in the event he defends himself very well from the start, and never becomes the target for bullying that his sister has been. At Fordlow one teacher, with the aid of two twelve-year-old monitors, teaches the class of forty-five, which has an age range from four to eleven. Reading, writing and arithmetic are the principal subjects. Though Laura can already read when she goes to school, she doesn't know the alphabet as such, and so is put into the babies' class to learn it by rote. When she comes to be tested for the Infants her literacy still goes unrecognized, and she is merely rebuked for gabbling her letters. She is reasonably successful at school, except in arithmetic and needlework. She and a friend, Emily Rose, act as unpaid assistants during the last two years of their school life. There are three teachers during this time: the first, Miss Holmes, is a traditionalist, believing in hard work, corrective discipline, and support of the established social order. The Rector reinforces these attitudes in his daily Scripture lessons. The next teacher, Miss Higgs, young and fresh from Training College, brings radical ideas of equality that in practice cause classroom chaos. Miss Shepherd, her replacement, provides something of a compromise: her discipline is rather shaky, but she tries to keep to the syllabus though her approach is innovatory. She encourages her pupils to make the best of their abilities by fostering their sense of self-respect, and by reading to them stories of self-made men.

bryony (*Bryonia cretica*), a climbing plant with poisonous berries.

A favourite amusement . . . called it See Chapter 23, where this is elaborated from an autobiographical viewpoint.

harmonium Musical instrument resembling a portable organ.

Royal Reader An anthology of extracts of poetry and prose.

Ivanhoe Historical novel published in 1819 by Sir Walter Scott (1771–1832), characterized by its vivid recreation of a chivalrous past, and featuring such heroes as Richard the Lion Heart and Robin Hood.

Prairie on Fire Presumably the description of the fire in the novel *The Prairie* (1827) by James Fenimore Cooper (1789–1851), author of *The Last of the Mohicans* etc.

Capture of Wild Horses An extract from a travel narrative, *A Tour of the Prairies* (1835), by Washington Irving (1783–1859), the American essayist, biographer and historian.

The Slave's Dream . . . Marmion Extracts from Scott's *Marmion* (1808). Lochinvar was the hero of the fifth ballad of the long poem.

Tennyson's Brook . . . Bells Alfred, Lord Tennyson (1809–1892) was created Poet Laureate in 1850. The extract from 'The Brook' usually included in anthologies begins with the lines: 'I come from haunt of coot and hern, / I make a sudden sally, / And sparkle out among the fern, / To bicker down a valley'. 'Ring out, wild bells' is from *In Memoriam* (verse 106), a long poem written in memory of his friend Arthur Hallam who died in 1833.

Byron's Shipwreck George Gordon, Lord Byron (1788–1824), a Romantic poet whose radical ideas and scandalous private behaviour brought him into disfavour with the English establishment, eventually causing him to go into voluntary exile. The description of the shipwreck comes from *Don Juan*, which in its entirety was later forbidden reading for Laura, on moral grounds (31,414).

Hogg's Skylark James Hogg (1770–1835), Scottish poet. A protégé of Scott, his verse celebrates Scottish country life, as in 'The Skylark'.

Lochiel's Warning A poem by Thomas Campbell (1777–1844), written in 1802. Lochiel was the chief of the Cameron clan.

Standard IV See *Setting*.

pot-hooks and hangers A reference to methods of forming curves in handwriting.

Old St Paul's Historical novel published in 1841 by William Harrison Ainsworth (1805–82). It is set in the time of the Great Plague and the Great Fire of London.

Little-Go An archaism for the first examination for the B.A. at Oxford and Cambridge. Used ironically here.

Like Gulliver ... Lilliputians A reference to the First Part of *Gulliver's Travels* in which the hero finds himself in a land of diminutive people.

Old Charley-wag! ... the bag 'Wag' was a nickname for 'Charles' in the nineteenth century, and this was a common derisive call (see *The Oxford Dictionary of Nursery Rhymes*, pp.116–17).

station fly A one-horse hackney carriage.

12, Her Majesty's Inspector

Note Misprint in Penguin Modern Classics. Both this chapter and the (correctly numbered) previous one are given as 'XI'.

The yearly visit of Her Majesty's Inspector of Schools is dreaded by teacher and pupils alike, though the majority of the school-children always pass the examination. Fortunately the Scripture Inspector has a different approach, and makes his visits seem almost like a social call. Both Laura and Edmund win the Scripture prize

– a *Book of Common Prayer* – in their respective years. The Squire at the Manor is unmarried: his mother Mrs Bracewell is therefore still Lady of the Manor; and she takes it upon herself to act as unpaid inspector of needlework at the school two or three times a year. As her circumstances become more reduced her manner becomes more overbearing; and Laura is one of several who regularly incur her wrath for poor work. The Squire himself is a more popular visitor, as he calls only once a year to arrange for some of the children to sing at his annual concert. The main event is always his Negro Minstrel Troupe, a group of village youths he has trained to form an accompaniment to his own banjo-playing and singing of Negro songs. Other items include piano pieces from young ladies of his acquaintance, and popular songs from the curate of the neighbouring village, who one year brought the stage down, literally, with his lively rendering of the polka. As the only public entertainment of the year, the event is fully attended and remains a topic for gossip for months afterwards.

gimlets Literally, small boring tools. Used here to emphasize his piercing gaze.

Victoria regia Gigantic water-lily of South American origin.

The Ancient Mariner *The Rime of the Ancient Mariner*, a long poem published in 1798 by S. T. Coleridge (1772–1834). It concerns the killing of an albatross by the mariner, the bad luck which follows, and his eventual penance and salvation. The line quoted is no.111, from Part 2 of the poem.

The standard must have been very low Mary Sturt, in *The Education of the People* (1967), offers contrary evidence that the standard set by many Inspectors was often terrifyingly high.

The Life of Moses Moses, Hebrew patriarch who led the Jews out of their captivity in Egypt.

law-giver Reference to the Ten Commandments (Exodus, 20,1–17).

Pisgah Mountain in Transjordan from which Moses viewed the Promised Land before his death (Deuteronomy, 3,27).

Little gallasses i.e. little devils who deserve hanging (from 'gallows').

Regency The years 1810–20 during which George, Prince of Wales (later George IV) acted as Regent, since his father George III was regarded as insane.

magic-lantern entertainment A pre-cinema technique of showing slides.

Primrose League Political association formed 1883 in memory of the Conservative politician Disraeli (1804–81), and devoted to the right-wing cause.

Darwin Charles Darwin (1809–82) published in 1859 *The Origin of Species* in which he put forward the theory that, contrary to the teachings of the Bible, man was not created but had evolved. In the popular imagination this was translated as meaning man had descended from the monkey.

13, May Day

May Day was the most important day of the year from the children's point of view, though the May garland was all that remained of the traditional festivities. The 'garland' was a bell-shaped wooden structure about four feet high, closely covered with flowers gathered on the last day of April. At six o'clock on May Day morning all the children aged between seven and eleven would assemble at the school to put the finishing touches and to place a china doll known as 'the lady' at the top of the garland. It was then hoisted aloft on a broomstick and the May Queen and her retinue in full regalia would set out in procession, calling at the Rectory and the Manor House, the farmhouse and the cottages, singing their May songs and collecting money according to the circumstances of the occupants. The route covered was about seven miles in all, including all the big houses of the surrounding area, where the children were often teased by the servants as part of the fun. The May Day money was shared out at school next day.

old May Day festivities References to May Day celebrations exist in English literature from early times and are particularly common in 16th-century writing.

turned turtle Overturned.

five-bob bit A crown, a silver coin worth twenty-five new pence.

14, To Church on Sunday

This chapter considers the part played by religion in the lives of the people of the hamlet. There is one Catholic family (at the inn) and three Methodist. Laura and Edmund are sometimes allowed to go to the Methodist Sunday evening meetings. The majority of the hamlet claims to be Church of England, though few regularly go to church. The motives of those who do attend are rather mixed, the desire for worship coming low on the list. The Rector himself in his sermons is more concerned with instilling acceptance of the established social order, than with his parishioners' spiritual salvation. Practical morality in the hamlet consists of a dislike of lying and stealing and a readiness to help those in illness or trouble.

The Rector visits each cottage once a year, his daughter calls more regularly. Neither is popular, though neither realizes it; Laura's mother is the only one to greet Miss Ellison with any warmth. After 1885, the Rector engages a series of curates to help him with his work. The most memorable are the scholarly Mr Dallas; Mr Alport, an ex-medical student; and the saintly Mr Marley. An account is given of Mr Marley's relationship with the end house family over several years.

piscina Stone basin in which communion vessels were rinsed.

the General Election of 1886 Won by the Liberals under Gladstone, though his triumph was short-lived, as his support of Home Rule for Ireland split his party and caused the fall of his Ministry.

genuflexions Bendings of the knee in worship.

Angelus bell Bell rung morning, noon and evening from Roman Catholic churches.

In my Father's house are many mansions From John, 14,2; quoted here by the grandfather to indicate his belief that Christianity is open to more than one interpretation.

Matthew, Mark, Luke and John An old Catholic nursery prayer, the 'White Paternoster' used to charm the bed and guard against the powers of evil during the night (see *The Oxford Dictionary of Nursery Rhymes*, pp.303–5).

Cromwell Oliver Cromwell (1599–1658), leader of the Parliamentary forces during the Civil War, and Lord Protector of England, 1653–8.

Napoleon Napoleon Bonaparte (1769–1821), famous French general who became Emperor of France. He was finally defeated by Wellington at the Battle of Waterloo in 1815.

Civil War i.e. between Royalists and Roundheads (1642–51). The battle of Naseby was fought in Northamptonshire in 1645.

Sankey and Moody's Hymn-Book i.e. *Gospel Hymns* collected by Ira David Sankey (1840–1908) and Dwight Lyman Moody (1837–99), American evangelists.

a la-de-da i.e. a pretentious person (featured in a comic song of 1880, which mocked affected pronunciation).

St Paul's injunction (See Romans, 12,15.)

Ruskin's road-making at Oxford John Ruskin (1819–1900), a leading socialist intellectual who – as part of their practical education – took Oxford undergraduates out road-building.

Anglo-Catholic Member of a group which held that the Church of England was a branch of the Catholic Church.

ulsters Overcoats.

The Imitation of Christ An edition of *De Imitatione Christi* by Thomas à Kempis (c.1380–1471), German monk and religious writer, called after his birthplace, Kempen.

St Francis of Assisi Italian friar (1181?–1226), founder of Fransiscan order whose rules stressed poverty for its members.

Dick Turpin English highwayman (1706–39), whose riding exploits were romanticized in William Ainsworth's *Rookwood* (1834).

Martha like Martha was the sister of Lazarus and Mary, friend of Christ (Luke, 10,38–42). In Christian allegory, she symbolizes practicality as opposed to her reflective sister Mary.

15, Harvest Home

Here the public festivals are described. The character of the religious holidays differ. Christmas Day is spent quietly at home with the family; Fordlow Feast, in September – held to celebrate the dedication of the church five hundred years before – is a noisier affair, which has transferred itself largely to Lark Rise and more specifically, to the Inn. The festivities last two days, the Sunday and the Monday. The Sunday provides a chance for the men to enjoy themselves eating and drinking on the proceeds of their Harvest earnings; the Monday gives their wives the opportunity to entertain relatives from nearby villages.

On Palm Sunday, houses are decorated with willow catkins as a 'palm' substitute, and the children traditionally eat figs. November the Fifth, Guy Fawkes' Night, is celebrated mainly by the boys. Everyone enjoys the festive bustling air that accompanies Harvest time, though the work is gruelling. Every year, after the harvest has been gathered in, the farmer provides an open-air Harvest home dinner, to which all the farm labourers and their wives are invited. But even this is eclipsed by the festivities of 1887, held to celebrate the Queen's Golden Jubilee. (This year marked the watershed of the old way of life of the hamlet; and the chapter ends with a bleak look into the future and the changes brought by the twentieth century.) Eleven of the young men of the hamlet die in the First World War: among them is Edmund.

bands of mummers Actors in a traditional folk play usually featuring St George, the Turkish Knight, the Doctor and Captain Slasher, though there were many regional variants (see Thomas Hardy's *The Return of the Native*, Book 2).
unked Dialect term meaning strange or troublesome.
swathes i.e. rows of mown corn.
Balmoral Castle ... John Brown Highland retreat of the Royal Family. The Queen's fondness for her attendant (or 'gillie') John Brown caused malicious comment. He rarely left her side during the twenty years preceding his death in 1883.
Esau's share i.e. a small share (see Genesis, 25,29–34).
Osborne Osborne House on the Isle of Wight was one of Queen Victoria's favourite residences.
Eton suit A short black jacket, open at the front, and matching trousers. Named after the famous public school.
Gallipoli ... Ypres Areas of battles that involved appalling casualties in the First World War (1914–18), in the Dardenelles (Gallipoli); Iraq (Kut-el-Amara); Northern France (Vimy Ridge); and Belgium (Ypres).

Revision questions on *Lark Rise*

1 Describe the hamlet of Lark Rise. How did the people manage to live on ten shillings a week?

2 What do we learn of the end house family from Chapters 1 and 2?

3 Describe the life of the men (a) at work (b) at leisure.

4 Who were the old people the child Laura knew well? Why did she enjoy their company so much?

5 How did the women spend their day?

6 Give an account of the callers at the hamlet.

7 What opportunities existed for (a) the boys (b) the girls, in terms of employment once they had left school?

8 Describe: (a) the children's games; *or* (b) the May Day walk; *or* (c) the public festivals.

9 How did Laura get on when she went to school? Why was the Inspector's visit feared?

10 What part did religion play in the lives of the people of the hamlet?

Over to Candleford

16, As They Were

Following the success of *Lark Rise* Flora Thompson was urged by her publishers to write a sequel, and *Over to Candleford* appeared two years later in 1941. The opening chapters provide a general description of the hamlet and its ways, and deals particularly with the end house family. Many of the details will already be fresh in the minds of present-day readers who have the advantage of reading the three books as one unit. In this chapter the geographical, historical and social background is re-established.

Readers are reminded that Lark Rise is a small hamlet in the wheat-farming country of north-east Oxfordshire. Victoria is on the throne and the country is at peace; but many of the young men still enlist as soldiers for a time before settling down on the land. The hamlet-dwellers, mostly farm labourers, regard themselves as being mid-way between the 'real poor' of the city slums on the one hand, and the rich gentry on the other. Social divisions are still very marked: the hard day of the agricultural poor is contrasted with the pleasure-seeking activities of the gentry, symbolized by the hunt galloping through the field the men are ploughing. But it is a society on the brink of change. The children's father, for example, rejects the idea of social superiors by refusing to allow Edmund to tug the forelock, or Laura to curtsey, as they have been taught at school. Similarly Frank, the local cricketer, is more amused than abashed by the suggestion that his team of 'amateurs' should be invited to play the 'young gentlemen' only if they let them win.

Other signs of change are more tangible than those of attitude. Bicycles begin to make their appearance, superseding the old country custom of walking everywhere, and newspapers replace the Bible as the written authority. But in day-to-day domestic details, life carries on largely as it has always done, and country customs still prevail.

hardbake Almond toffee.
Arcadian Referring to Arcady or Arcadia (from Arkadia, a mountainous district of Greece), which has become equated in literature with an ideal of rustic simplicity and happiness.
Christie's Old Organ* and *Froggy's Little Brother Touching tales of street arabs were common in the popular literature of the time. The former was by Mrs O. F. Walton and the latter (published in 1875) by 'Brenda' (Mrs Castle Smith).
He himself ... Alma i.e. 20 September 1854, the first battle of the Crimean War (1854–6).
Sebastopol City in the Ukraine. Strategic base besieged for almost a year in the Crimean War.
ferrule Metal cap.
Florence Nightingale (1820–1910), founder of modern nursing, and celebrated for her devoted work in the Crimean War.
Jonah ... swallowing A dreadful pun, since the Old Testament records that the Hebrew prophet Jonah was swallowed by a 'great fish' Jonah, 1,17.

17, A Hamlet Home

The reader's attention is focused on the family at the end house. Here, Laura, Edmund and their father, all outsiders in the hamlet in their various ways, are described. Some of Laura's earliest memories, of the house itself and of people and scenes, are recorded, the most striking being the recollection of an evening after a pig-killing.

billycock hat Bowler hat.
scratchings i.e. crackling, the bits of pork fat left after making lard.
ragwort (*Senecio jacobaea*); a native British plant, with yellow flowers and a tough stem; common on waste ground.
whorls Spirals.
routed i.e. turned over the earth with its snout, looking for food.
sweetbread The pig's pancreas.

18, 'Once Upon a Time'

Laura's mother is vividly recollected, together with her wonderful gift for narrative. Some of her tales are pure invention, others are family stories that have been handed down. She also entertains her children at bedtime by singing old ballads to them, or by describing the delights of Candleford where their richer relatives live. A visit to Candleford is a long-promised treat, but something always seems to happen that postpones it.

A pocket Venus A popular term for someone small and beautiful (Venus being the Goddess of Love in Roman mythology).
Australian goldfields Between 1851 and 1870, a series of gold discoveries was made in New South Wales, Victoria and Queensland.
Chancery A division of the High Court of Justice, concerned with questions of estate, inheritances etc. (see Charles Dickens's *Bleak House*, (1852–3).
chimera i.e. illusion.
J.P. Abbreviation for Justice of the Peace.

19, 'A Bit of a Tell'

This chapter is concerned with the neighbours the child Laura knows well. Her favourites are the old countrywomen Queenie, Old Sally, and Mrs Prout (see Chapter 5). Her mother's chosen friends tend to be rather genteel and, from the child's point of view, boring – since their conversation is mainly confined to their pregnancies (Mrs Massey); their daughters in service (Mrs Hadley); and their health (Mrs Finch). Laura prefers to eavesdrop on the good-natured gossip of the uninvited casual callers: Rachel who drops in 'for a tell'; the slightly mysterious Patty, formerly a publican's widow but now (apart from her fondness for drink) a model wife to young Amos; and the feather-brained Gertie. The most haunting in appearance and manner is Mrs Merton, whose melancholy airs foreshadow the tragic events of her later life. The women talk mainly of their own affairs and those of their hamlet neighbours. They have little time for politics and no real interest in the lives of the local gentry, though they seem to derive some sense of satisfaction from having aristocratic 'neighbours' in the area. The barriers were too rigid to allow for inter-class personal relationships; though occasionally a young lord or lady would be more approachable, and some old nurses or ladies' maids became, after long service, true friends of their employers.

A Bit of a Tell i.e. a gossip.
smelling-salts Scented ammonium carbonate, usually carried in small decorative bottles, to relieve faintness.
ax i.e. ask.
fuzz i.e. furze.
The golden ball . . . lifetime i.e. good luck comes to everyone at least once.
Board of Guardians Governing body of the workhouse.
potations Drinks.
gowk A variant of 'gawk' meaning an awkward or bashful person.
stillroom maid One who catered for the light refreshments.
chaw-bacon A contemptuous term for a country bumpkin.
the very spit i.e. exact likeness.
hugger-mugger i.e. hushed up, confusedly. Presumably a hasty marriage because the girl was pregnant.
the Tragic Muse Melpomene, one of the nine Goddesses who presided over the Arts and Sciences according to Greek and Roman mythology.
Hell-Fire Club A club for dissolute young men of means at the beginning of the eighteenth century.
in the godspeed i.e. at the end.

20, Mrs Herring

A lively account is given of the visit of the genteel Mrs Herring, the landlady from Candleford who has been asked by Laura's father to clear the built-in cupboard in the children's room of things left in storage so that the end house family could use the extra space to build a separate bedroom for Edmund. The children have great pleasure in seeing the cupboard, long a source of terror to the imaginative Laura, emptied of its contents. Laura is amused to witness the personality clash between Mrs Herring and her mother, and the disparity in social graces at teatime between Mrs Herring and her husband. She is rather more upset by Mrs Herring's dismissive treatment of the inquisitive Rachel, though Rachel herself is relatively unperturbed. The chapter ends happily with the news from the children's father that they are going soon to make Mrs Herring's trip in reverse, and will at long last go 'over to Candleford' to visit their relations.

Ananias and Sapphira Ananias and his wife Sapphira were both struck dead because they had lied to God in trying to deceive Peter (Acts, 5,1–10).

Tusmore House See *Setting.*

to come hail-fellow-well-metting me i.e. to come greeting me so familiarly.

21, Over to Candleford

The end house family go 'over to Candleford' for the day in the pony-cart borrowed from the inn-keeper. They are met on the outskirts of the town by their smartly-dressed cousins, Ethel, 13, and Alma, 12, who accompany them on the remainder of their journey. Uncle James Dowland is a builder with a thriving business, and a person of some importance in Candleford. He is a church-warden and a member of many committees, including that of the temperance movement, to which he recruits Laura and Edmund. Aunt Edith, kind but ineffectual, is seemingly in awe of her husband and daughters. The family live in extremely comfortable circumstances and the hamlet children are very impressed by the size and luxury of the house and the lavish hospitality offered. But Laura is not entirely at ease, partly because she feels her family are patronized by her cousins, and partly because the whole experience is too overpowering for a child of her sensitivity.

a measley old screw Measley (usually spelt measly) is a slang term for worthless; a screw is a vicious horse.

chip Woody fibre split into thin strips.

leghorn hats Hats made from fine plaited straw, imported from Leghorn in Italy.

equipage Carriage and horses with attendants. Used slightly ironically here.

wistaria (or wisteria, *Wisteria floribunda*) A climbing plant, usually with blue, purple or white flowers.

Churchwarden A lay officer elected annually to assist the Vicar.

commode A chair or box containing a chamber pot.

Band of Hope An association which aimed at indoctrinating children against drink while they were young.

Ramsgate Popular holiday resort on the Kent coast; in Laura's time it was a genteel watering-place.

potpourri Jar containing dried petals and spices.
Ireland . . . Gladstone says See other references in notes on Chapters 1, 4, and 14.
Lord Harrington says Misprint for Lord Hartington (1833–1908), nicknamed 'Harty-Tarty'. Anti-Home Rule (see following note).
Joey Chamberlain Joseph Chamberlain (1836–1914), famous radical Lord Mayor of Birmingham (1875) who became an MP in 1876 and was President of the Board of Trade in Gladstone's government (1880–5). In 1886 he left the Liberal Party because he was opposed to the policy of Home Rule for Ireland favoured by Gladstone.

22, Kind Friends and Relations

The mother and children join the father at the house of their other Candleford relations, Aunt Ann, Uncle Tom, and their five children. Uncle Tom, a bootmaker with his own business, is a liberal both in politics and philosophy, so the end house children find their father restored to good humour in such congenial company, and visibly relaxing over a glass of beer while settling the Irish question to his apparent satisfaction. Laura and Edmund play with their cousins, Molly, Annie, Nelly, Amy and Johnny the youngest; and everything pleases Laura that afternoon. The chapter ends with the author's memories of Johnny over many years, pampered as he then was, but fated to suffer terribly in the First World War.

Froggy's Little Brother See notes on Chapter 16.
a snob Dialect term for a cobbler.
herring-boning A kind of cross-stitching.
Kut See notes on Chapter 15.

23, Sink or Swim

Soon after the trip to Candleford Laura begins school, as described in Chapter 11. Here the reader is told how she copes socially rather than academically. On the walk to school the Lark Rise children see much bullying, once of an old tramp encountered on the road, often of the more timid such as Laura. One girl in particular, Ethel Parker, makes her life a misery for years; ironically when encountered in adult life, in Bournemouth, Ethel speaks fondly of their happy childhood times together. As Laura grows older, she finds it easier to make friends at school; and the more definite pleasures of friendship include receiving other girls' confidences, as well as blackberrying with them, picking flowers, making daisy-chains, and sliding on the ice – though this last activity once nearly proves fatal.

bullifant A word combining the meaning of bull and elephant, customarily used to mean a large, clumsy person, but used approvingly here.
toy dog A lap dog.
the wicked . . . green bay-tree See Psalm 37,35.

24, Laura Looks on

Still on the subject of school, various unusual events interrupting classroom routine are recorded – the coming of the German band once a year, the passing of a grand funeral, the General Election, the Bishop's consecration of an extension to the churchyard followed by tea at the schoolmistress's cottage for Laura. Her life is generally easier from a social point of view after Edmund begins school, and their mutual pleasures on the way home are described. Above all, they share a love of literature, particularly of the Psalms and the works of Scott. They both write stories and poems, an activity frowned upon by their mother as a waste of Laura's time, which she feels can be better spent mastering such skills as sewing, then regarded as an essential part of a girl's education. A short discourse on changing fashions concludes the chapter.

Home, Sweet Home A song by the American actor and playwright John Howard Payne (1791–1852), with music by Sir Henry Rowley Bishop (1786–1855). It contains the famous refrain 'Be it ever so humble, there's no place like home'.
factotum Man of all work, general servant.
Ministering Children A popular collection of moral tales about 'good' children by Maria Louisa Charlesworth, published in 1854.
Waverley Novels A series of thirty-two novels and tales by Sir Walter Scott (1771–1832).

Old St Paul's See notes on Chapter 11.
The way . . . was cold Scott's *The Lay of the Last Minstrel* begins, 'The way was long, the *wind* was cold'.
Charge, Chester . . . on From Scott's *Marmion*, Canto Sixth verse 31.
stays Corsets.
It's a corker to me i.e. it amazes me.

25, Summer Holiday

The visit to Candleford (Chapters 21 and 22) sets a precedent for future summers – the pony and cart being hired one fine Sunday each year. The summer that Laura is eleven and Edmund nine their mother is expecting a baby, and it is arranged that the two children should walk 'over to Candleford' by themselves and stay with Aunt Ann, Uncle Tom and their cousins for the period of the confinement. The pleasures of the walk and of the visit itself are described. Though not wealthy people, Uncle Tom and Aunt Ann live in much more comfortable circumstances than the children's parents, and various differences in domestic detail are given to make this point. The chapter includes a character sketch of the orphan boy Benny, who helps in the shop, and of Bertha, the maid at Aunt Edith's who was kind to Laura on her first visit to Candleford. Laura's mother has her baby, a girl, and on the last day of the holiday the children go up to the attic to play charades. Laura is delighted to find many books there, and is invited by Uncle Tom to read to him in his workshop.

Livingstone David Livingstone (1813–73), Scottish missionary and explorer who discovered the Victoria Falls in 1855.
corn-crake Bird with harsh grating voice, found in cornfields.
cockchafers Large flying beetles.
carking Burdensome.
charades Usually a game where participants act a word for an audience to guess.
Pamela, or Virtue Rewarded See notes on Chapter 6.
The Pilgrim's Progress See notes on Chapter 2.
Cranford (1853), a novel by Mrs Gaskell dealing with a peaceful English village, inhabited chiefly by genteel old ladies (e.g. Miss Matty).
one of that kidney i.e. one of that kind.

26, Uncle Tom's Queer Fish

Laura becomes a regular summer visitor to her cousins' house in Candleford and continues to read to her uncle in the afternoons. There are constant interruptions, partly business ones but mostly social, for Uncle Tom has many friends. The most memorable from Laura's point of view are: the 'queer fish' – Miss Constance, the wealthy recluse who lives alone apart from her nineteen cats; the poet who walked from a nearby village where he has rented a cottage for the summer; the socialist doctor bent on reform; the aristocratic Mr Mostyn, tormented by doubts about conversion to Catholicism; finally, the young commercial traveller with his marital problems.

inverness cloak Cloak with a detachable cape covering the shoulders.
these eagles of his ... or rue Evidently the poet was fond of allegory.
Norfolk suit Informal loose-fitting suit (photographs of Bernard Shaw often show him wearing one).
Newman John Henry Newman (1801–90), a leading intellectual of the day who had been converted to Catholicism.
Methinks ... too much Adapted quotation from *Hamlet*, III,2,225.
Didymus (c.310–c.395). A blind Christian theologian, i.e. Tom will not 'see' his viewpoint.
old enchantress i.e. the Roman Catholic Church.
Lucy Snowe's ... Frenchman A reference to Charlotte Brontë's *Villette* (1853).

27, Candleford Green

On one visit to Candleford Laura goes with Edmund and her cousin Molly to visit her mother's friend Dorcas Lane, who keeps the Post Office at Candleford Green, a village nearby. The children particularly look forward to seeing the 'telegraph machine' which they have often heard their parents talk about. At Candleford Green the children go their separate ways. Edmund explores the blacksmith's forge, which forms part of the house. Molly joins the maid Zillah in the garden, while Laura enjoys the company of Dorcas Lane, who takes her on a conducted tour of the old house. We are told something of Dorcas' background and character; of how she runs the joint business of post office and forge, the latter with the help of her foreman Matthew, and three journeymen who 'live in'. The chapter ends with a look into the future when the blacksmith will adapt to the demands of the twentieth century and begin to specialize in motor repairs.

Battle of Waterloo This took place on 18 June 1815.
Greenwich time Standard time in Great Britain, and from which the whole world adapts its clocks.
The Times Founded in the eighteenth century and traditionally thought of as the most authoritative daily paper.
Darwin See notes on Chapter 12.
farriery Treatment of sick horses.
Black Beauty A popular name for a horse after the publication in 1877 of the book of that title by Anna Sewell (1820–78).
fichu A small triangular shawl, worn round neck and shoulders.
poke bonnet Bonnet with projecting rim.

28, Growing Pains

The 'growing pains' referred to in the chapter-heading are the problems of Laura's early teens, classic in their way. At home she begins to feel the effects of overcrowding, as there are five children in the end house by the time she is twelve. At school she and another girl, Emily Rose, are alone in Class 1, which means in practice that they do their lessons and the domestic chores in the schoolmistress's cottage. To Laura it seems that Emily Rose has everything she lacks: exceptional attractiveness of appearance and character; success at schoolwork; the status of an only child adored by indulgent parents; even an assured future with a doting husband – her childhood sweetheart Norman. When Laura leaves school to help at home full-time she feels she is moving into an increasingly isolated position. She has little freedom, while her mother seems preoccupied, overworked and unable to relate to her as she can to the smaller ones. Her mother is clearly disappointed in her ambitions for both her elder children: Edmund refuses to be an apprentice carpenter, and she regards Laura as an inadequate nurse. Her depression and moodiness continue until one November day, having run out into the fields in a temper, she suddenly finds the natural beauty of the scene exercises its old healing effect on her spirits: she feels instinctively that this source of renewal will be hers for as long as she lives.

Class I Presumably the equivalent of Standard 5 (see *Setting*).
hassock A cushion (for kneeling on in church).
nainsook Soft, shiny cotton material.
Ministering Children See notes on Chapter 24.
Queechy*, or *The Wide, Wide World *The Wide, Wide World* (1850) and *Queechy* (1853) were written by Elizabeth Wetherell ('Susan Warner'), 1819–95. Both feature young heroines who lead fairly adventurous though virtuous lives.
speedwell eyes i.e. blue eyes (after the flower).
moral Likeness.
fin de siècle Literally 'end of the century', used generally to mean slightly decadent.
Hindhead See *The author and her work*.
Swinburne Algernon Charles Swinburne (1837–1901), unconventional poet and man of letters.
Omar Khayyám A Persian poet (d.1123). His *Rubáiyát*, as translated by Edward Fitzgerald (1809–83), was considered daring reading in the 'nineties because of its emphasis on sensual pleasure as the chief aim of living.
as yellow as ... ague Tropical diseases, such as malaria, caused discolouration of the skin, and shaking as with a fever (an ague).
land-girl A reference to the Women's Land Army, which came into being in the First World War.
hag-rid i.e. haunted, under stress.

29, Exit Laura

After Laura's experiences at the end of the previous chapter, she sees her mother in a new light, and their relationship becomes much easier. But they are soon to be parted. In the spring, Dorcas Lane writes from Candleford Green offering Laura work at the post office, and in early May she leaves Lark Rise in the hired pony-cart to begin her new life in Candleford Green.

Revision questions on *Over to Candleford*

1 What steps does Flora Thompson take to keep the title of *Over to Candleford* relevant to this part of the trilogy?

2 Write a character sketch of any *two* members of the end house family from the evidence offered in Chapters 17 and 18.

3 Which of the neighbours did Laura find interesting? Write a short description of not more than *three* of the characters you have chosen, using only details found in this part of the trilogy.

4 Compare and contrast (a) Uncle James Dowland and Uncle Tom (b) Aunt Edith and Aunt Ann (c) the cousins at each house.

5 Give an account of the difficulties experienced by Laura in her early teens. How were they resolved?

Candleford Green

30, From One Small World to Another

Laura leaves home at fourteen-and-a-half to take up a post as assistant to Miss Dorcas Lane at the Candleford Green post office (see Chapter 27). Here we are told of her first day there. She already knows Miss Lane to be a kind and generous friend; she is now impressed by her air of authority and efficiency in the conduct of her domestic and business affairs. Laura is, generally very pleased with her new surroundings, and is specially impressed by the luxuriant garden with its three wells, and by the fact that she has her own bedroom. Only the prospect of having to be 'sworn in' before a Justice of the Peace next morning prior to beginning work casts a shadow over her enjoyment of the day.

molern See notes on Chapter 5.
pestle and mortar Club and bowl (often used for pounding herbs).
Banbury cakes Local cakes – pastry filled with a currant mixture.
conundrums Riddles.
he's a seven-stunner i.e. he weighs seven stones.
capers A bramble-like South European shrub; the flower-buds are pickled for culinary use. ('English capers' are pickled nasturtium seeds.)
Solomon's seal A plant with drooping green-and-white flowers.

31, On Her Majesty's Service

Laura's interview with Sir Timothy, the J.P., is more pleasant than she has anticipated. Back at the post office, though at first she finds the array of forms and stamps bewildering, dealing with them gradually becomes less confusing. She soon manages to give change correctly and begins to enjoy her work, particularly when meeting people. The hours are long, but the busy periods intermittent and the general pace of business leisurely. The daily routine begins at 7 o'clock with the arrival of the morning mail from head office brought by Thomas Brown, the evangelical postman. And in the course of her duties, Laura learns to operate the telegraph instrument. Twice a year the head postmaster Mr Rushton comes from Candleford to audit the accounts and to make a general inspection. These 'surprise visits' are in fact well organized in advance and are combined with a social call. One very great pleasure of Laura's new life is that she has access to a far wider range of literature than previously. At first she reads the books left to Miss Lane by her father; later she obtains a library ticket to the Mechanics' Institute at Candleford.

The 1d and the ½d ... half-sovereigns Obsolete coins 1d = 1 old penny; 10s = 10 shillings (a shilling = 5 new pence); a sovereign = £1.
japanned Covered with hard varnish.
MFH Master of Foxhounds.
morning suit Grey tailcoat and grey trousers (usually worn with a grey top-hat).
Sabbatarian principles i.e. belief in devoting Sunday strictly to worship.
Cooking and Household Management First published in volume form in 1861 by Isabella Mary Beeton (1836–65). Basically a reference book, like the following two.
The Complete Farrier Presumably for Matthew's use. William Gibson was generally regarded as the authority on this subject.
Dr Johnson's *Dictionary* Authoritative dictionary published in 1755 by Samuel Johnson (1709–84).
Hume's *History of England* David Hume, the Scottish philosopher and historian (1711–76), published his *History of Great Britain* in several volumes in the period 1754–61.
Cowper's poems ... *Seasons* Eighteenth-century poets who drew on nature for much of their subject matter: William Cowper (1731–1800); Thomas Campbell (see notes on Chapter 11); Thomas Gray (1716–71); James Thomson (1700–48). *The Seasons* was written in four parts between 1726 and 1730.
Byron's *Don Juan* See notes on Chapter 11.
The Origin of Species See notes on Chapter 12.
Mechanics' Institute Mechanics' Institutes were first established in the early nineteenth century to provide opportunities for self-education for working men. Later, membership became more general.
Charles Dickens (1812–70), the great 19th-century novelist (see Chapter 33).
Barchester Towers (1857). One of the best known novels in the Barsetshire Series by Anthony Trollope (1815–82).

Pride and Prejudice (1813) by Jane Austen (1775–1817).
his surname ... maternal ancestor A pun incorporating the meanings of 'hussy' and 'virago', both names for bad-tempered or badly behaved women, the caretaker's name being Hussey.

32, The Green

Laura finds the physical and social structure of the village of Candleford Green very different from that of the hamlet of Lark Rise. The post office is on the quiet side of the Green, so Miss Lane and later Laura are able to observe the activities on the busier opposite side, occupied by the shops. The Green itself is the focus of attention once a year when the Hunt meets there. Character sketches are given of some of the villagers of that time, Dr Henderson, Mr and Mrs Coulsdon (the vicar and his wife) and the deaf-mute, 'Luney Joe'. (Joe ended his days in the County Asylum after his mother died, which prompts some general comment on the plight of the sick poor in those days: The common practice was to rely on the charity of relations or the better-off.) Recollections of old culinary arts and of the luxury of bath-night finish off the chapter.

stirrup-cup A glass of wine etc. drunk while on horseback before the Hunt begins.
that the first covert ... drawn i.e. that a fox would be flushed from the first lair approached.
out-running the constable i.e. only one step ahead of the law.
in queer street i.e. in financial difficulties.
vapourish Prone to fainting and hysteria.

33, Penny Reading

Laura finds that the village life includes many social activities. Sewing parties are held separately for the cottagers (the Mothers' Meetings) and for the more well-to-do. Both these groups have 'outings' in the summer, as do the choir and the Sunday school children. Extracts from the works of Dickens (read by old Mr Greenwood), and from *Uncle Remus* (read by the American Mrs Cox) are among the popular items at the monthly Penny Reading.

The Church Social, with its light refreshments and indoor games, breaks the monotony of the winter months and gives an opportunity for the more fashion-conscious to 'dress-up'. One year, Laura is escorted home from the Church Social by a young reporter Godfrey Parrish, temporarily employed on the local paper. Though they never meet again, they continue to write to each other for some years.

Miss Lane's main social offering is her yearly 'hay-home' supper, given after the hay in her two paddocks has been cut by a Mr and Mrs Beer. Miss Lane invites to this supper all the people who have worked for her in any capacity during the year. It is a traditional pork supper with plenty of home-made wine, followed by songs from all present.

Another traditional event at Candleford Green is the Village Feast, which is always a general holiday. The green is turned into a fairground for the occasion; and the merry-go-rounds, swingboats and various side-shows usually attract a large crowd.

Happidrome A cinema. This allusion would be more readily picked up by Flora Thompson's original readers, as *Happidrome* was a popular radio show during World War II.

Uncle Remus *Uncle Remus, His Songs and His Sayings* (1880), a collection of folk tales told to a small white boy by Uncle Remus, an old negro servant; written by Joel Chandler Harris (1848–1908).

Excelsior . . . Hesperus Published in *Ballads and Other Poems* (1841) by Henry Wadsworth Longfellow (1807–82).

The Heart of Midlothian Historical novel by Scott (1818).

Vanity Fair (1847–8) by William Makepeace Thackeray (1811–63).

Alexandra See notes on Chapter 10.

An' Sal 'aved nation well i.e. and Sal behaved extremely well (nation being a euphemistic abbreviation of 'damnation', here meaning 'very' or 'extremely').

an' sprig 'ee up i.e. smarten you up.

gwain Going.

Plough Monday The first after Epiphany (6 January).

memento mori Reminder of death (Latin).

Childe Harold *Childe Harold's Pilgrimage*, a long narrative poem concerning a romantically world-weary hero, published between 1812 and 1818, by Lord Byron (see notes on Chapter 11).

34, Neighbours

The dwellings clustered round the Green are a mixture of shops and private homes. Opposite the forge, the three Williamses, father, son and grandson, carry on a long established carpentry business. The two elder Williamses uphold the family traditions of music and craftsmanship; Willy is less committed. He and Laura become good friends, as he shares her love of literature. He is killed in the Boer War, and when soon afterwards his father and grandfather die, the shop is demolished to make way for a builder's showroom. Another friend of Laura's lives next-door to the carpenters – Mrs Macey, the slightly mysterious postwoman. She ekes out her wages by taking in needlework, to support herself and her young son Tommy. Two extremes of private housing are represented by the home of Mr Repington, a rich and courteous old gentleman who entertains Laura at the post office with riddles; and the cottages, mainly occupied by manual workers and farm labourers. 'The Stores', next-door to Mrs Macey, is a drapery business run by the Misses Pratt, Pearl and Ruby. Their mother is a permanent invalid and their father, an ex-commercial traveller, is more famous for the regularity of his drinking habits and his unexplained disappearance for a year than for his business sense. Adjoining 'The Stores' is a grocery, 'Tarman's', and a bakery run by Mr and Mrs Pratt and their large family. The few remaining shops scattered around the Green include that owned by the old dame who sells prunes, rice and toffee.

Time, like an ever-rolling stream ... away Line from the famous hymn 'O God, our help in ages past'; written by Isaac Watts (1674–1748).

habitués Habitual visitors.

Dante Gabriel Rossetti (1828–82). English poet and painter of Italian parentage, and founder-member of the Pre-Raphaelite Brotherhood.

indentures Contract binding an apprentice to a master.

hobble-de-hoy Clumsy youth.

Between the shabby old covers ... Duty Poems by John Keats (1795–1821), Percy Bysshe Shelley (1792–1822), and William Wordsworth (1770–1850).

soldier's grave ... South Africa i.e. he died in the Boer War (1899–1902), 'veld' being the open grasslands of South Africa.

Freemasons A kind of secret society, the members of which assist each other, and their dependants, in time of stress.

valet Personal servant.

'a little pennicking bit of a woman' i.e. a tiny person. Adjectival use of 'pinkeen', meaning a little fish.

35, At the Post Office

Apart from its business purpose, the post office functions as a social centre. Sir Timothy frequently stays for a chat with Miss Lane, and once his wife Lady Adelaide embarrasses Laura by asking her to join the Primrose League. Laura loves listening to stories and in the course of her work she hears many stirring descriptions of service in India from the Army pensioner 'Old Ben'; and many strange tales, such as the history of the antique tapestry posted one day by 'Long Bob', the lock-keeper at the canal. Sometimes she is required to be a more active participant in her customers' affairs. Usually the Post Office closes at eight, but in the late summer Miss Lane authorizes Laura to sell postal orders to the Irish harvesters after official hours, so that they can send part of their week's money home to Ireland. One or two of her 'regulars', being illiterate, ask her to write the accompanying letters to their dictation; and she is impressed by their fluency and charm. She often performs a similar service for the gipsies, who call for their letters since there is no delivery to their tents or caravans. In return for her letter-writing Laura's fortune is told by one old gipsy, Cinderella Doe. Laura derives a great deal of pleasure from the ordinary everyday transactions of the post office. She enjoys the friendship of the cottagers, the bright and breezy manner of the gentlemen farmers, and the high-spirited behaviour of the cycling club who keep her busy sending telegrams on some Saturday afternoons. A brief account of the advent of the bicycle is given, and the chapter ends on a note of unrepentant female chauvinism.

Timbuctu Town in West Africa, often cited in the past as an example of a remote place.

Primrose League See notes on Chapter 12.

Daily Citizen . . . Daily Herald Liberal and Labour newspapers.

'every boy and every girl . . . little Conserva*tive* Lines from the comic opera *Iolanthe* (1882) by W. S. Gilbert (1836–1911) and Sir Arthur Sullivan (1842–1900).
cobbled their garments i.e. patched up their clothes.
Queen Bess's day Queen Elizabeth I reigned from 1588 to 1603.
bulls i.e. contradictory statements, sometimes known as 'Irishisms'.
froxy High-spirited, frisky.
fait accompli i.e. thing done, rendering further argument useless (French).

36, 'Such is Life!'

Various features of village life are commented upon. No serious crime takes place in Candleford Green. Occasionally there may be a case of poaching or theft, but on the whole there is little work for the local constable. Most contention arises within families, as in the much debated marital dispute between Sam and Susan, and the legal wrangle over inherited land between 'Old Jim' and his niece. Gossip is rife – mostly harmless, but sometimes scandalous. The more malicious element in the village also enjoys sending anonymous 'comic' Valentines – Laura is upset by this practice one year. Education had played a part in banishing many of the old superstitions, for instance those concerning witchcraft; but superstition lingers on in several of the local cures for ailments. A typical 'walking funeral' is described, and belief in the supernatural is touched upon. In this context is included the thought-provoking story narrated to Laura by her mother of the extrasensory perception of a dying cousin.

affiliation case i.e. a legal case to establish paternity of (and financial responsibility for) an illegitimate child.
pigwash Pigswill.
testator's fancy Wish of person making a will.
the Scab From 'scabies', a skin disease.

37, 'Ta-ra-ra-boom-de-ay!'

On the whole Laura enjoys a carefree existence at the post office. She likes the work and is happy living with Miss Lane. Zillah's grumblings amuse rather than perturb her, and Matthew and the younger smiths are clearly fond of her. Though she looks forward eagerly to the weekly news and 'treats' from home, the pull of her new life is strong. She feels excited by the new horizons opening up to her, glimpsed through the conversation of the friends of her own age in the village. Her mood is perfectly summed up by the refrain of a song popular at the time, and it seemed that her own high spirits are reflected in all around. The only thing that occasionally saddens her is the loss of her old 'freedom of the fields'.

lafeting Laughing, light-hearted.
black ox i.e. old age.
hoity-toity i.e. superior, 'stuck up'.
blued Whitened by use of a blue powder in laundering (often contained in a muslin bag known as a blue bag).
The Quiver . . . Home From 1854 onwards, the Religious Tract Society published periodicals, such as *The Sunday at Home* (1854–1940), which in their tone and content steered a course between religious works and popular fiction.
monthly parts Most of Dickens's novels were originally published in serial form.
Daily Telegraph First London daily penny paper, founded in 1855.
Queechy . . . World See notes on Chapter 28.
Ouida Pen-name of Marie Louise de la Ramée (1838–1908) who wrote colourful romances, with risqué morality, set in high society.
Girls' Own Paper (1880–1908). The sister-paper of *Boys' Own Paper*, published by the Religious Tract Society.
the trial of Oscar Wilde Oscar Wilde, famous writer and wit (1854–1900). He was a leading member of a movement advocating 'art for art's sake', and after being found guilty of homosexual offences, served a prison sentence from 1895 to 1897.
Yellow Book Avante-garde journal launched in 1894 with Aubrey Beardsley as art editor. Wilde was popularly believed to have been carrying a copy of it when he was arrested.
Answers (1888–1956). Popular paper containing snippets of general information, founded by Alfred Harmsworth.
Tit-Bits A rival paper on similar lines, begun by George Newnes in 1881 and still in publication.
to talk prunes and prisms i.e. to talk in a prim and proper way.
Miss Lotty Collins's . . . Ta-ra-ra-boom-de-ay Usually billed as

Lott*ie* Collins (1866–1910). The song, which ends with a can-can style dance, was first sung at the Tivoli Music Hall in 1891, and swept three continents during the 1890s.

38, Letter-Carrier

Laura becomes a postwoman after Mrs Macey leaves the Post Office to join her husband in London. She is delighted by her new appointment, though she meets with some initial opposition from her parents when she goes home for the weekend to obtain their permission. Only two problems mar her total happiness at being out in the countryside again: the cows which block her way, and the rough teasing she has to put up with from Sir Timothy's footmen. The former she learns to cope with, but the latter always remained a trial. Male attention of another kind comes from the young gamekeeper Philip White, who eventually proposes to her. Laura's refusal gratifies Miss Lane enormously, and she entertains hopes that Laura will stay permanently at Candleford Green. But the concluding lines of the chapter make clear that this is not to be so.

indeed the winter of their discontent An adaptation of the opening lines of Shakespeare's *Richard III*.
Quite the prodigal . . . calf Ironical allusion to the story of the Prodigal Son (*Luke*, 15,11–32).
ha-ha A sunken fence or ditch dividing lawns from rough pasture.

39, Change in the Village

The village is gradually becoming a suburb of the nearby town. The transition is accentuated by the death of the old vicar, Mr Coulsdon, who has supported traditional ideas of social hierarchy; and by the arrival of the new vicar Mr Delafield. From the first he refuses to stand on his dignity, and meets his parishioners very much as their equal. He makes no secret of his poverty and lets his children run around barefoot to illustrate the point. His preaching is as revolutionary as his attitudes, both in its colloquial style and in the everyday morality of its message.

Higher wages for the agricultural worker help to hasten social change. This is reflected in the occupancy of the villas rapidly being built on the outskirts of the village. The Green family gives Laura her first introduction to lower-middle-class attitudes and aspirations, of which we are told, somewhat ominously, 'she was to see a great deal later'. The book ends with Laura's thoughts on the last morning of her postwoman's round, as she prepares to leave Candleford Green and her beloved countryside.

terracotta Brownish-red.
whaleboned up to the ears i.e. tightly corseted.
Diamond Jubilee Celebration in 1897 of sixty years of Queen Victoria's reign.
éclat Brilliance, renown; here the meaning is 'social distinction' (French).
there was ... dressing-tables One with a movable mirror.
Laura thought ... two boys, perhaps Flora Thompson's family consists of two boys and a girl. Winifred becomes a nurse, Basil emigrates to Australia and Peter, the youngest, is killed in the Merchant Navy during the Second World War (see *Purely for Pleasure*).
Marie Correli Pen-name of Mary Mackay (1855–1924), an extremely popular romantic novelist, famous for her sensational plots.
Nat Gould Nathaniel Gould (1857–1919), American journalist and novelist who wrote about 130 novels, all concerned with horse-racing.

Revision questions on *Candleford Green*

1 What were Laura's first impressions of her new life at Candleford Green?

2 Describe a typical day at the post office from Laura's point of view.

3 How did Candleford Green differ from Lark Rise?

4 Write a character study of Miss Lane, paying close attention to *two* episodes in which you consider Flora Thompson portrays her most vividly.

5 Describe the friendships Laura made in Candleford Green.

General questions

1 How would you defend *Lark Rise to Candleford* as a work of literary merit, rather than as a document chiefly of use to the social historian?

2 How far do you agree with H. J. Massingham that the trilogy is 'the story of the irreparable calamity of the English fields'?

3 'People were poorer . . . but they were happier.' How does Flora Thompson develop this theme in *Lark Rise*?

4 'The small scene, so commonplace and yet so lovely, delighted her' (28,384). Discuss this quotation with reference to either (a) nature *or* (b) society as viewed by Flora Thompson in either *Over to Candleford* or *Candleford Green*.

5 'The trilogy's weakness is a structural one – it lies in the failure to weld three totally distinct books into an artistic whole.' Discuss.

6 '*Over to Candleford* and *Candleford Green* provide a poor sequel to the achievement of *Lark Rise*.' Discuss.

7 'The portrayal of the end house family is the book's most attractive feature.' Discuss, with reference to at least *two* members of the family.

8 Flora Thompson has been praised for her sympathetic presentation of character. Do you think this praise is justified? Illustrate your answer by reference to not more than *three* individuals (excluding the end house family).

9 What contribution does the setting make to the trilogy?

10 Write an essay on the main features of Flora Thompson's style, indicating what appeals to you most.

Pan study aids Titles published in the Brodie's Notes series

W. H. Auden Selected Poetry

Jane Austen Emma Mansfield Park Northanger Abbey Persuasion Pride and Prejudice

Anthologies of Poetry Ten Twentieth Century Poets The Poet's Tale

Samuel Beckett Waiting for Godot

Arnold Bennett The Old Wives' Tale

William Blake Songs of Innocence and Experience

Robert Bolt A Man for All Seasons

Harold Brighouse Hobson's Choice

Charlotte Brontë Jane Eyre

Emily Brontë Wuthering Heights

Robert Browning Selected Poetry

John Bunyan The Pilgrim's Progress

Geoffrey Chaucer (parallel texts) The Franklin's Tale The Knight's Tale The Miller's Tale The Nun's Priest's Tale The Pardoner's Tale Prologue to the Canterbury Tales The Wife of Bath's Tale

Richard Church Over the Bridge

John Clare Selected Poetry and Prose

Samuel Taylor Coleridge Selected Poetry and Prose

Wilkie Collins The Woman in White

William Congreve The Way of the World

Joseph Conrad The Nigger of the Narcissus & Youth The Secret Agent

Charles Dickens Bleak House David Copperfield Dombey and Son Great Expectations Hard Times Little Dorrit Oliver Twist Our Mutual Friend A Tale of Two Cities

Gerald Durrell My Family and Other Animals

George Eliot Middlemarch The Mill on the Floss Silas Marner

T. S. Eliot Murder in the Cathedral Selected Poems

Henry Fielding Joseph Andrews

F. Scott Fitzgerald The Great Gatsby

E. M. Forster Howards End A Passage to India
Where Angels Fear to Tread

William Golding Lord of the Flies The Spire

Oliver Goldsmith Two Plays of Goldsmith: She Stoops to Conquer; The Good Natured Man

Graham Greene Brighton Rock The Power and the Glory

Thom Gunn and Ted Hughes Selected Poems

Thomas Hardy Chosen Poems of Thomas Hardy
Far from the Madding Crowd Jude the Obscure
The Mayor of Casterbridge Return of the Native
Tess of the d'Urbervilles The Trumpet-Major

L. P. Hartley The Go-Between The Shrimp and the Anemone

Joseph Heller Catch-22

Ernest Hemingway For Whom the Bell Tolls
The Old Man and the Sea

Barry Hines A Kestrel for a Knave

Gerard Manley Hopkins Poetry and Prose of Gerard Manley Hopkins

Aldous Huxley Brave New World

Henry James Washington Square

Ben Jonson The Alchemist Volpone

James Joyce A Portrait of the Artist as a Young Man

John Keats Selected Poems and Letters of John Keats

Ken Kesey One Flew over the Cuckoo's Nest

Rudyard Kipling Kim

D. H. Lawrence The Rainbow Selected Tales Sons and Lovers

Harper Lee To Kill a Mockingbird

Laurie Lee As I Walked out One Midsummer Morning
Cider with Rosie

Thomas Mann Death in Venice & Tonio Kröger

Christopher Marlow Doctor Faustus Edward the Second

W. Somerset Maugham Of Human Bondage

Arthur Miller The Crucible Death of a Salesman

John Milton A Choice of Milton's Verse Comus and Samson Agonistes Paradise Lost I, II

Sean O'Casey Juno and the Paycock
The Shadow of a Gunman and the Plough and the Stars

George Orwell Animal Farm 1984

John Osborne Luther

Alexander Pope Selected Poetry

Siegfried Sassoon Memoirs of a Fox-Hunting Man

Peter Shaffer The Royal Hunt of the Sun

William Shakespeare Antony and Cleopatra As You Like It
Coriolanus Hamlet Henry IV (Part I) Henry IV (Part II)
Henry V Julius Caesar King Lear King Richard III
Love's Labour Lost Macbeth Measure for Measure
The Merchant of Venice A Midsummer Night's Dream
Much Ado about Nothing Othello Richard II Romeo and Juliet
The Sonnets The Taming of the Shrew The Tempest
Twelfth Night The Winter's Tale

G. B. Shaw Androcles and the Lion Arms and the Man
Caesar and Cleopatra The Doctor's Dilemma Pygmalion Saint Joan

Richard Sheridan Plays of Sheridan: The Rivals; The Critic; The School for Scandal

John Steinbeck The Grapes of Wrath Of Mice and Men & The Pearl

Tom Stoppard Rosencrantz and Guildenstern are Dead

J. M. Synge The Playboy of the Western World

Jonathan Swift Gulliver's Travels

Alfred Tennyson Selected Poetry

William Thackeray Vanity Fair

Flora Thompson Lark Rise to Candleford

Dylan Thomas Under Milk Wood

Anthony Trollope Barchester Towers

Mark Twain Huckleberry Finn

Keith Waterhouse Billy Liar

Evelyn Waugh Decline and Fall Scoop

H. G. Wells The History of Mr Polly

John Webster The White Devil

Oscar Wilde The Importance of Being Earnest

Virginia Woolf To the Lighthouse

William Wordsworth The Prelude (Books 1, 2)
Wordsworth Selections

W. B. Yeats Selected Poetry

Australian titles

George Johnston My Brother Jack

Thomas Keneally The Chant of Jimmie Blacksmith

Ray Lawler Summer of the Seventeenth Doll

Henry Lawson The Bush Undertaker & Selected Short Stories

Ronald McKie The Mango Tree

Kenneth Slessor Selected Poems

Ralph Stow The Merry-Go-Round in the Sea To the Islands

Patrick White The Tree of Man

David Williamson The Removalists

Student's notes

Student's notes